PRAISE FOR
LIBERATION FRONT

"For a number of years now I have admired Kemper Crabb's work with music. Now I hear he is branching out into wordsmithing, and I look forward to seeing what that will bring."

—Doug Wilson, pastor, theologian, and author

"Over the course of the last three decades, I have my known my friend Kemper Crabb to be one of the most remarkably creative, notoriously well read, fiercely orthodox, delightfully insightful, and resolutely visionary men of our day. I feel an anxious, anticipatory stirring whenever he undertakes a new project—certain that he will once again feed my soul just as surely as he will rattle my nerves."

—George Grant, pastor and author

"Endorsing Kemper Crabb is one of the easier things I've been asked to do. While his leading of worship at our church is exceptional, his preaching and teaching may be even better. He plumbs the depth and breadth of God's Word and makes it clear to his listeners, opening up minds to the mind of Christ. I always look forward to hearing new songs he has composed and now I can look forward to a new book."

—Reagan Cocke, priest at St. John the Divine Episcopal, Director of Adult Education and Assistant Rector

"Music, mentoring, teaching, blogging: I've watched Kemper Crabb for decades, and I have been profoundly blessed. His is a unique voice, a fresh take, a perspective that stands apart from the rest. I love his passionate concern for the things of God. I love his inventive blend of old and new. I love his mastery of a wide variety of very diverse creative forms. In short: Kemper Crabb? I'm a fan."

—Diana Pavlac Glyer, award-winning author of *Clay in the Potter's Hands* and *The Company They Keep: C. S. Lewis and J. R. R. Tolkien as Writers in Community*

LIBERATION FRONT
RESURRECTING THE CHURCH

KEMPER CRABB

A POST HILL PRESS BOOK
ISBN (hardcover): 978-1-61868-821-7
ISBN (eBook): 978-1-61868-820-0

LIBERATION FRONT
Resurrecting the Church
© 2016 by Kemper Crabb
All Rights Reserved

Cover Design by Randy Rogers

Post Hill

PRESS

Post Hill Press
275 Madison Avenue, 14th Floor
New York, NY 10016
posthillpress.com

A SHORT NOTE TO THE READER

In past centuries, the English language was written using capitalization for the initial letters of the Titles and Names of God, of His Attributes and all words which pertained to Him, and even of important concepts generally. Though this practice died a gradual death in the wake of the standardization of spelling and type-setting, I've found that reading books from before that time communicate a respect and reverence for God that have largely disappeared as God in the years since has increasingly been seen as only a projection of the human mind, or as a being only slightly different from mankind.

The older writings tend to force the modern reader to consider the Person and Actions the Lord with more deliberation than is normally the case today, in my opinion. I've consequently chosen to adopt that older approach to capitalization in this book, in the desire that you, the reader, will likewise be driven to a deeper and more thoughtful contemplation of Christ Jesus and the ideas associated with His Kingdom presented here. I also hope this approach won't put the reader off, but will instead help move him to accept and act on what is written.

Kemper Crabb

This book is dedicated to Kemper and Tommye Crabb, from whom this fruit is not far fallen.

CHAPTER 1

THE SEVEN MODES OF THE CHURCH

We are here because of a Story. A true Story. This Story involves despair and betrayal, joy and loyalty, heroism and cowardice, the blackest hatred and the highest love, murder and sacrifice, fear and trust, adventure and challenge, unremitting vengeance, catastrophe and eucatastrophe (the Good Catastrophe, which is what makes this story a comedy rather than a tragedy).

This Story is behind every other story written or told or depicted, every song ever written or poem chanted, every battle fought; every empire and government, every market place, every scrap of learning, science and technology, every nanosecond of history.

This Story is the cause of all your dreams and desires, the things you love and value, it gives meaning to everything because you were made for the Story and the Story for you. The Story is still going on, it is not finished, and both you and the Story were made by God for His Pleasure.

Before time, the Father and Son gifted Each Other the Church. History (wars, cosmos, stars, Adam & Eve) exists for this meaning, and from this meaning. You, as an individual, and us together, all exist from and for the meaning of this Story.

What was the Gift? The Church. A people. A nation both in and beyond history forever. This Gift, the Church, is the central institution of history—the Colony of Heaven. The Church lives in history, going through all kinds of things good and bad-seeming, and all the time God is forming us into an eternal Gift for Himself.

Here's the deal:

If you are a Christian, you are a part of that Story. You are part of the Church.

Everything that ever happens in history—the thing that gives history meaning, not just to your life and mine, but to everybody's life, whether they're good or evil, whether they burn forever as a horrible monster, or whether they shine forever with the Glory of God—is all about the Story, and the Gift of the Church is at the center of that Story.

The Early Church told the persecuting pagans they should be glad the Church existed, because the only reason the world, pagans included, existed was so God could have the Church. They were right.

The Old and New Testament Church across thousands of years, all those people were doing one thing: they were living out the Story. Like them, you have a part in that Story. It is your Story, not just God's. He made it so you would have a part in the Story and that is more important than anything you'll ever do or value or want.

The funny thing is that the only way you'll ever be who you're supposed to be, the only way you'll truly have satisfaction or joy, the only way you'll be who God made you to be, is if you take your place, the place created for you from the beginning, your place in that Story.

Step into who the Church is. If you don't, my brothers and sisters, you will waste your life.

> Then Jesus said to His disciples, "If anyone desires to come after Me, let him deny himself, and take up his cross, and follow Me. For whoever desires to save his life will lose it, but whoever loses his life for My sake will find it. For what profit is it to a man if he gains the whole world, and loses his own soul? Or what will a man give in exchange for his soul? For the Son of Man will come in the glory of His Father with His angels, and then He will reward each according to his works." (Matthew 16:24-27).

You've heard this before. "What was Jesus thinking?" you may be asking yourself. If Jesus wanted followers, why didn't He make it easier? All that denial of self and losing your life stuff is really sort of a downer. I mean, there are all these things you want to do.

This is a radical demand that Jesus lays out here, and the Church's history is replete with those who thought it too radical and demanding. Why would anybody want to do this? Lose their life to find it. It sounds insane. You'd have to be a madman to do that. So why is this a good deal?

Because of the Story. We're here because of this Story. The world itself is here because of this Story. It's a really wild Story.

"You lose your life to gain it" means you lose your empty, dark, self-generated, self-referential story to enter Christ's Story, for which He made you. He *made* you for His Story.

His Story, as it is lived out beneath the canopy of Heaven, is all about the Church. Most of us don't think much about the Church because we're only thinking about ourselves, about how "Me and Jesus, we've got our own thing going", and Church is just where all of us who have our own things goin' with Jesus just hang out together, so we can maybe help each other have our own personal thing going with Jesus.

We suffer through hanging out with other people in church, trying to make it as comfortable for ourselves as possible, thinking that the use of Jesus' Name will help justify our self-seeking.

To miss this Story is to miss everything. There are numbers of people who hang out on the edges of the Story, who sit in church, but don't engage. Jesus calls them chaff, and at the End of the Age the Angels will come and reap the wheat, but first they take out the chaff.

> Whose fan is in his hand, and he will thoroughly purge his floor, and gather his wheat into the garner; but he will burn up the chaff with unquenchable fire (Matthew 3:12, KJV).

Chaff is part of the Story, but it is not the good part of the Story; it's the bad part, because, see, chaff is only good for burning. You don't want to be chaff. We are, in the pages to come, going to look at the Church in ways you might not have considered in any depth.

Why is this important to you? Because you *are* the Church.

The Church is the Colony of Heaven. It's not just you alone; it's us together, living out the Story of Christ together on the Earth, before the Face of God. And it is us becoming together and individually who we were meant to be.

In case you missed it earlier, let me say this again: you will never become who you were meant to be unless you do so in the context of, against the background of, in the middle of, the Church.

You're not going to do it on your own, I guarantee you, because you were made to be part of God's people. That's how God has created and plays out His Story with His people. There are, of course, individuals in His People; you, as an individual, are part of His people, and have a place among His people. But if you're thinking of yourself as separate from His Church, you're wrong.

The buildings you go to are not the Church. *You* are the Church. The Church, all of us Christians here, meet in buildings, but *we* are the Church *together*. That's one thing you should realize.

The other thing is that the Church is not just a place you go, but it's a way you *are*. That's what we aim to learn about in the pages to come: being the Church—doing the Story.

The Story changes the world.

There's a short saying from classical education: Know the Good; Love the Good; Do the Good, which is really saying Know God; Love God; Obey God.

When you do that, folks, you'll find the oddest thing happens. You have to give up your life to do that, to *lose* your life.

But you'll find you have more real life than you ever thought possible.

How would I know? When I was fifteen years old God showed Himself and changed me, and ever since that day I've been trying to learn how to lose my life. It's been the greatest adventure I've ever known. I've been deeply fulfilled. I've suffered, and it's been worth every nanosecond of suffering. It's been great.

I'm writing this because I want you to know I serve the Story, and I want you to serve the Story, and I want you to serve the Church and the Lord of the Church, because that's what is going to set you free, and nothing else is ever going to set you free. I promise.

The Church (and therefore you, Christian) exists in at least seven modes, or states of being. It's always helpful to know what we are.

The Church is Romance

> For I have betrothed you to one husband, that I may present you as a chaste virgin to Christ (2 Corinthians 11:2b).

What is this about? ROMANCE.

That verse is about how God loves the Church. This verse is about God Who loves you in the way that someone loves their fiancé.

God loves His people in a dedicated, single-minded fashion, and He wants them to remain pure for Him, because He knows that if they do that, they'll be fulfilled in Him. That's romance, folks.

The Bible says that every couple you've ever know who are married and in love are imaging out Christ and His love relationship to the Church. It says this because Jesus loves the Church like the most passionate couple you've ever known love each other, and more, because He does it perfectly.

> Wives, submit to your own husbands, as to the Lord. For the husband is head of the wife, as also Christ is head of the church; and He is the Savior of the body. Therefore, just as the church is subject to Christ, so let the wives be to their own husbands in everything. Husbands, love your wives, just as Christ also loved the church and gave Himself for her, that He might sanctify and cleanse her with the washing of water by the word, that He might present her to Himself a glorious church, not having spot or wrinkle or any such thing, but that she should be holy and without blemish. So husbands ought to love their own wives as their own bodies; he who loves his wife loves himself. For no one ever hated his own flesh, but nourishes and cherishes it, just as the Lord does the church. For we are members of His body, of His flesh and of His bones. For this reason a man shall leave his father and mother and be joined to his wife, and the two shall become one flesh. This is a great mystery, but I speak concerning

Christ and the church. Nevertheless let each one of you in particular so love his own wife as himself, and let the wife see that she respects her husband (Ephesians 5:22-33).

Every love story you've ever read or heard about, everything you thought was truly romantic finds its roots in this: God has revealed to the world He has an Undying Love for the church. For you.

Pagans try to make romance about something else, but, at bottom, the romance in the world is about the fact that God loves His people. Romance. One of the things the Church is about. There's more.

The Church is a Family

Not only is the Church about romance, the Church is a Family.

But as many as received Him, to them He gave the right to become children of God, to those who believe in His name: who were born, not of blood, nor of the will of the flesh, nor of the will of man, but of God (John 1:12-13).

For as many as are led by the Spirit of God, these are sons of God. For you did not receive the spirit of bondage again to fear, but you received the Spirit of adoption by whom we cry out, "Abba, Father." The Spirit Himself bears witness with our spirit that we are children of God, and if children, then heirs-

-heirs of God and joint heirs with Christ, if indeed we suffer with Him, that we may also be glorified together (Romans 8:14-17).

Both of these passages are about family. The Church is a Family. God loves His Church, His people in the way that you love the family members that you love in your family, even the one you love most. But that's not all.

The Church is a Body

He is the image of the invisible God, the firstborn over all creation. For by Him all things were created that are in heaven and that are on earth, visible and invisible, whether thrones or dominions or principalities or powers. All things were created through Him and for Him. And He is before all things, and in Him all things consist. And He is the head of the body, the church, Who is the beginning, the firstborn from the dead, that in all things He may have the preeminence (Colossians 1:15–18).

…and not holding fast to the Head, from whom all the body, nourished and knit together by joints and ligaments, grows with the increase that is from God (Colossians 2:19).

This means the Church is a Body, a Body of which Christ is the Head. Just like your head is on your body, that's His relationship to the Church. It's so organic, it's so connected, it's so intertwined, that just as your head directs your body, but they are still one thing, that is how Christ's Relationship is to the Church.

The Church is about Romance, the Church is about Family and the Church is a Body, of which Christ Jesus is the Head.

> For as we have many members in one body, but all the members do not have the same function, so we, being many, are one body in Christ, and individually members of one another (Romans 12:4-5).

> Now you are the body of Christ, and members individually (1 Corinthians 12:27).

This means that you (ya'll, which is actually what the original Greek in this verse says) are members of Christ's Body. From before the beginning of time, the One who made time saw you as part of His body; indeed, He constructed history around the Story so you *would be* a part of His Body.

You are to obey Him as your body obeys your head. You'll notice we are also members of one another (Romans 12:5). The Church is a Body.

The Church is about Romance. The Church is a Family. The Church is a Body.

These are not just pictures; they're not just metaphors. They're more real than virtually anything else you'll ever know. This is the Truth, not just some poetic word-picture someone made up: this is the Truth.

These are the central Truths in light of which you need to live your life. Romance, Family, and Body. What else?

4 The Church is a Temple

Do you not know that you are the temple of God and that the Spirit of God dwells in you? (1 Corinthians 3:16).

And what agreement has the temple of God with idols? For you are the temple of the living God. As God has said:

"I will dwell in them
And walk among them.
I will be their God,
And they shall be My people."
(2 Corinthians 6:16).

What happens in a temple? You worship in it. In India, there are temples everywhere, as there are pagan temples in all pagan lands.

Now, therefore, you are no longer strangers and foreigners, but fellow citizens with the saints and members of the household of God, having been built on the foundation of the apostles and prophets, Jesus Christ Himself being the chief corner*stone,* in whom the whole building, being fitted together, grows into a holy temple in the Lord, in whom you also are being built together for a dwelling place of God in the Spirit (Ephesians 2:19-22).

So you, and all of us together, are being built together into a Temple in which the God who created and holds all things together, who was before the world, lives. He *lives* in us.

Pagans in India are sometimes afraid of Christians because they know (they frequently can tell) that their God lives *in* them.

We are built into a Temple to live out the worship of God to spread the fragrance of the incense of the Colony of Heaven in the Earth before God and before the tribes of mankind.

The Church is a Romance. The Church is a Family. The Church is a Body. The Church is a Temple.

Again, not just word pictures: the real deal. The Word of God: "To the law and to the testimony! If they do not speak according to this word, it is because there is no light in them" (Isaiah 8:20).

The Church is the Pillar and Ground of Truth

"I write so that you may know how you ought to conduct yourself in the house of God, which is the church of the living God, the pillar and ground of the truth" (1 Timothy 3:15).

The Church of the Living God is the Pillar and Ground of the Truth. People across the world seek truth. The Church is the place truth comes from, the instrument God uses to further His Truth.

The Church is who preaches the Gospel they've been entrusted with, and who are to live out its patterns in such a way that the shape of the Church provides a context and backdrop to the preaching of the Gospel so that hearers can take it seriously and believe it.

You are the arena in which God reveals His Truth to the world: the Pillar and the Ground of the Truth.

The Church is about Romance. The Church is about Family. The Church is a Body. The Church is a Temple. The Church is the Pillar and Ground of the Truth.

The Church is a Weapon

> And I also say to you that you are Peter, and on this rock I will build My church, and the gates of Hades shall not prevail against it (Matthew 16:18).

Now I've heard preachers, again and again in my life, read this passage and say, "See? See? We're safe! They can't get us! The gates of Hell can't get us!"

It is true that the gates of Hell can't get us, but let me ask a question: Have you ever heard of anyone in all of history attack with their gates? Nobody attacks with their gates. Gates are for defense. Gates are *attacked*.

This passage is about a Church that is beating down the very gates of Hell. This is not some little wimpy, retreatist Church hiding off in the corner. This is a Church that is aggressively attacking and destroying the works of the Devil.

> For this purpose the Son of God was manifested, that He might destroy the works of the devil (1 John 3:8b).

And Jesus said something really arresting:

> "Most assuredly, I say to you, he who believes in Me, the works that I do he will do also; and greater works than these he will do, because I go to My Father" (John 14:12).

Do you believe that? Do you? This is what the Church is here to do. Because the church is a Weapon.

The Church is about Romance. The Church is a Family. The Church is a Body. The Church is the Pillar and Ground of the Truth. The Church is a Temple, and the Church is a Weapon.

> For I consider that the sufferings of this present time are not worthy to be compared with the glory which shall be revealed in us. For the earnest expectation of the creation eagerly waits for the revealing of the sons of God. For the

creation was subjected to futility, not willingly, but because of Him who subjected *it* in hope; because the creation itself also will be delivered from the bondage of corruption into the glorious liberty of the children of God. For we know that the whole creation groans and labors with birth pangs together until now. Not only *that,* but we also who have the first fruits of the Spirit, even we ourselves groan within ourselves, eagerly waiting for the adoption, the redemption of our body (Romans 8:18-23).

What is this passage talking about? The destiny of the created world is tied up with the Church, and on the Day the Church completes its task, when God fulfills His Purposes in the Church, the entire universe will be liberated because the Church is completed.

7 The Church is a Liberating Army

To me, who am less than the least of all the saints, this grace was given, that I should preach among the Gentiles the unsearchable riches of Christ, and to make all see what is the fellowship of the mystery, which from the beginning of the ages has been hidden in God who created all things through Jesus Christ; to the intent that now the manifold wisdom of God might be made known by the Church to the principalities and powers in the heavenly places, according to the eternal purpose which He accomplished in Christ Jesus our Lord (Ephesians 3:8-11).

The principalities and powers are the angelic beings who run and rule over reality. One of the purposes of the Church is to demonstrate to these creatures, both evil and otherwise, the Purposes of God, the Story. The Story I started telling you about. The fullness of the Story was not going to be revealed until the Church came about, and now the Church is telling and living out the Story in front of these Principalities and Powers. That is, to say the least, cosmic!

The Church exists to embody and make known, even to the Satanic "principalities and powers in the heavenly places", the liberation accomplished through Christ Jesus and His Redemption. The Church bears witness to this liberating truth even to fallen angels. For this, the Church (and therefore, you) was formed.

I don't know what you want from life. I don't know what you want, but I can't think of anything that anybody *would* want in their whole lives that is not fulfilled in one of these categories.

What are you looking for? To make a difference with your life? How about liberating the world?

What are you looking for? Romance? You'll never find a love as deep as the one that Jesus has for the Church.

What are you looking for? Truth? It's only found in the Christ "in Whom are hidden all the treasures of wisdom and knowledge" (Colossians 2:3).

What are you looking for? Excitement? What could be more exciting than being a weapon against Satan's dark kingdom?

What are you looking for? To belong somewhere? How about the Family God prepared for you which stretches across time and eternity?

What are you looking for? To help by contributing to something larger than yourself? Nothing could ever be more helpful or effective than taking up the functions for which you were created in the Body of Christ.

What are you looking for? To experience mystery and the reality of the spiritual realm? What could have more impact in this area than being yourself indwelt by God as a Temple, as one small Temple being joined across time and space to a greater Temple of millions of others?

What are you looking for? What is it that you're holding on to, that you're afraid you're not going to get by abandoning yourself to the life of God's People, the Church? Whatever you're looking for, you're only going to find in the bosom of the Lord Jesus Christ's Body, in His people as He walks in among and through them.

For through Him we both have access by one Spirit to the Father. Now, therefore, you are no longer strangers and foreigners, but fellow citizens with the saints and members of the household of God, having been built on the foundation of the apostles and prophets, Jesus Christ Himself being the chief cornerstone, in whom the whole building, being fitted together, grows into a holy temple in the Lord, in whom you also are being built together for a dwelling place of God in the Spirit" (Ephesians 2:18-22).

The Church is the Liberation Front. It changes the world. It is the instrument of the Kingdom, in which is found freedom and life.

You are the Revolution. You are the Church. You are the Liberation Front. Don't you think it is time we started to actively live what we are? If you do, you'll find that you lose your life to truly find it in the midst of the Story.

In the chapters which follow, we'll examine in more detail the meaning and impact of these seven modes of being as the Church.

Come and join us.

Come and be the Liberation Front. Come and be the Church.

CHAPTER 2

THE FOUR MARKS OF
THE CHURCH

The Church is (1) Romance, (2) Family, (3) Body, (4) Temple, (5) Ground and Pillar of the Truth, (6) Weapon, and (7) Liberating Force, as we saw in the last chapter. Unless your life is developed in the shape of these seven things, you will never be who you were created to be in God's Story. You were created to be formed fully into the shape of these seven things.

Most of us can remember such non-essentials as the lyrics to songs on the radio, actors and actresses and their movies and marriages and public statements, etc., and even the names of a good number of athletes and their team histories and individual statistics. Yet we have difficulty remembering these seven basic categories which form the core description of the most important things in our lives.

I would venture to guess this is because of the level of importance we assign to things. We always remember the things that are most important to us, after all. I would also venture to suggest that we elevate the importance of these seven categories in our estimation to at least the level of importance of a pop song or an actor's name, so we might remember these central categories of our existence.

Of course, we don't have to do so, but I would guess that when push comes to shove, and God, in His Mercy, begins to shape us aggressively into these modes, and it starts hurting, and we're confused, and don't know why it's happening, it would help us more than the lyrics of a pop song, or the name of an athlete, to remember that God is trying to set us free by forcing us into these modes that reflect Him.

These modes of being are some of the most important things in our lives, so we should try to remember these seven things and see ourselves constantly in light of them, because we *are* the Church, and are therefore, both personally and all together, being formed by the Lord into more perfect embodiments of the things we already are in Christ, things which progressively free us. Just a suggestion, of course.

The Colony of Heaven

You hear people upset about colonialism these days (in most cases, deservedly so). Why? Because a colony or colonialism is when a different group of people from the original inhabitants invade, move in, and set up a different government from the one before, and begin to rule in the name of, and by the authority and power of, the nation or government who sent the invading colony for the very purpose of extending their rule. This is not generally appreciated by those who were loyal to the former government that the invading colony displaced, frequently with some justification.

However, imagine the original government which the colony displaced was oppressive and evil (say, like Nazi Germany or Soviet Russia). This changes the perspective on colonialism considerably. The displacement of the oppressive government by the invading colonizers would, in fact, be a liberation, provided the colonial government was not evil and oppressive.

The earth fell under the oppressive rule of death and Satan's world-system at the Fall of Man in the Garden of Eden at the beginning of time (Genesis 3; Ephesians 2:2; John 10:10; Galatians 4:3). After millennia of that deadly rule, God invaded the world in the Person of Christ Jesus (Galatians 4:3-4), and redeemed a people, the Church, His Body, Who, after His Ascension into Heaven, would expand the beachhead of His Kingdom and colonize the world, displacing Satan's defeated kingdom.

You are Heaven's Colony. You are the living, breathing, walking Colony of God on earth. God has come into the world. He has invaded through the Lord Jesus, and is taking back what is His, which He did definitively at the Crucifixion, Resurrection, Ascension, and Enthronement of Christ, but He is extending His Reconquista (Re-conquest) through space and time by the proclamation and enactment of His Story and Kingdom in history by His Church.

He's living in *you*; He's walking, He's talking, He's breathing through *you*. You are the Colony, the outpost, the army of the In-breaking Kingdom of God, the Kingdom that hammers on the gates of Hell (Matthew 16:18). You are the interface between Heaven and earth. You are the way in which and through whom God primarily reveals Himself on the earth. You are the bearer of the Image of God (Genesis 1:28), being formed into the Image of Christ (2 Corinthians 3:12-18). You are part of a Colony—the Colony of Heaven. All the seven modes we've learned about are colonial categories for us.

Four Marks of Identity

What does the Church look like? Let's look at Acts 2:38-47:

Then Peter said to them, "Repent, and let every one of you be baptized in the name of Jesus Christ for the remission of sins; and you shall receive the gift of the Holy Spirit. For the promise is to you and to your children, and to all who are afar off, as many as the Lord our God will call." And with many other words he testified and exhorted them, saying, "Be saved from this perverse generation." Then those who gladly received his word were baptized; and that day about three thousand souls were added to them. And they continued steadfastly in the apostles' doctrine and fellowship, in the breaking of bread, and in prayers. Then fear came upon every soul, and many wonders and signs were done through the apostles. Now all who believed were together, and had all things in common, and sold their possessions and goods, and divided them among all, as anyone had need. So continuing daily with one accord in the temple, and breaking bread from house to house, they ate their food with gladness and simplicity of heart, praising God and having favor with all the people. And the Lord added to the church daily those who were being saved.

We learn here of Four Marks or Aspects which are necessary for the Church to *be* the Church, all of which are—not accidentally—necessary for Christian discipleship.

The situation being presented and commented upon here in Acts is this:

Jesus had finished His Earthly Ministry, and ascended into Heaven to be enthroned at the Right Hand of the Father. The 120 disciples were gathered in prayer and worship in the upper room, and the Holy Spirit had been poured out and given in a way He had never been given before, a way that revolutionized the lives of the people in that worship service in the upper room.

The Outpouring of the Spirit established what we normally think of as the New Testament Church, which in many ways is just an extension of the Old Testament Church of Israel, but is also new, in that, for the first time, the Church is open to *goyim*: to Gentiles who are neither ethnically Jewish nor have been circumcised.

Miracles began to happen: tongues of fire appeared over the Christians' heads, and they began to praise God, speaking languages they'd never learned, worshipping Him in many languages, showing that redemption is for all the earth's nations (and that every human language is a fit vehicle for praising the Lord). The 120 spilled out into the streets, ecstatically offering praise to God in the various languages they were supernaturally enabled to speak.

The multi-national visitors to Jerusalem for the Pentecost Festival were amazed, hearing God praised in their various languages, but the ecstatic nature of this outpouring of worship caused some to think the Christians were drunk. Peter, in response, said, "These people aren't drunk" (Acts 2:15), and began to deliver one of the greatest sermons ever preached to all the astounded onlookers, explaining that what they were seeing and hearing was the fulfillment of a prophecy tied to Jesus' Resurrection. Verses 38-40 of Acts 2 record the end of that message:

> Then Peter said to them, "Repent, and let every one of you be baptized in the name of Jesus Christ for the remission of

sins; and you shall receive the gift of the Holy Spirit. For the promise is to you and to your children, and to all who are afar off, as many as the Lord our God will call." And with many other words he testified and exhorted them, saying, "Be saved from this perverse generation."

Then are recorded the effects of Peter's preaching in verses 41-47.

Verse 41 tells us, "Then those who gladly received his word were baptized; and that day about three thousand souls were added *to them*." So, there were 120 believers before Peter's sermon, but there were 3,120 or so after it. Pretty good for a day's evangelism. It's in regard to these converts that the rest of the passage is concerned. If you want a good thumbnail sketch of what the Church should look like, verse 42 provides just that: "And they continued steadfastly in the apostles' doctrine and fellowship, in the breaking of bread, and in prayers. Then fear came upon every soul, and many wonders and signs were done through the apostles."

There are four things mentioned here that are Defining or Identifying Marks of the Church (and they're considerably more important than actors or athletes, so we should try to remember them):

1) The Apostolic Doctrine (or Teaching)
2) Fellowship

3) The Breaking of Bread
4) Prayers

Let's look at these Marks in greater detail.

1) The Apostolic Doctrine (or Teaching), in which verse 42 tells us these believers "continued steadfastly," e.g., they deliberately and constantly exposed themselves to, and heeded and acted consistently on what the Apostles taught. Of course, the Apostles doubtlessly taught about the Words and Life of the Lord Jesus (which informed the writing of the New Testament), and did so in light of the Old Testament Scriptures (since the New Testament had not yet been written, and also since they always taught and wrote quoting the Old Testament). Essentially, the Apostles were teaching God's Word, and the believers listened and obeyed it, and it changed their lives. They *continued* in the teaching of the Word.

"So Jesus was saying to those Jews who had believed Him, 'If you continue in My Word, then you are truly disciples of Mine; and you will know the truth, and the truth will make you free'" (John 8:31-32, NASB).

You'll note, before Jesus said what people are always quoting Him as saying ("You shall know the truth and the truth will set you free"), He said, "*If you continue* in

My Word, *then* you are truly disciples of Mine." These are *contingencies*, gentle reader. Only *if* you *abide* (the other frequent and accurate translation for the Greek word here), which is to say, hold to and live out His Word, only *then* are you one of His Disciples, the only ones who really know the truth, and only then will you be freed by the knowledge of His Truth.

The shape of your discipleship, the ground of knowing the truth which sets you free, is continuing steadfastly in Jesus' Word. Let us not kid ourselves here: truth is defined by Scripture. Anything that is at odds with the Bible is *not* truth; it is, rather, a lie. This is so because the God Whose Character and Being is the source of all truth is the One Who, in the Person of the Holy Spirit, has divinely inspired the Bible (2 Timothy 3:16-17; 2 Peter 1:19-21; Isaiah 8:20). This is also why, as Saint John Calvin once famously wrote, "the Scriptures are the lenses which correct our sin-distorted vision, and, to be free, we must gaze through those lenses, and act in terms of what we see there." Which is, of course, Jesus' point in John 8:31-32.

It is therefore important that we pay attention to God's Word, that we *study* it, that we *continue* in the Doctrine of the Apostles, who, after all, either wrote or discipled the others who wrote the New Testament under the Spirit's Inspiration. Thus, this first Defining Mark of the Church teaches us that the Church reads, studies, teaches, preaches, and *continues* in and lives out the Bible, which is the Apostles' Teaching, the first Mark of the Church.

2) Fellowship was continued in just as steadfastly as the Apostolic Doctrine, and is in fact the context in which they heard and continued in that teaching, and is consequently the second Defining Mark of the Church.

Most churches have a fellowship hall of one sort or another, which name stems from this passage (and similar others) where it addresses fellowship. What does it mean to continue in fellowship? It means they were a community of people who were committed to God and to each other, who lived their lives together and took care of each other. The rest of the book of Acts records the appointment of Deacons to make sure all were fed and cared for equally, and to help the sick. In the Early Church, Deacons even took the Communion to those too sick to attend services, and the Elders prayed for, taught, and anointed the sick with healing oil (James 5:14-15). As many of the believers were very poor, they even pooled their money to make sure all had what they needed (as verses 44-45 of Acts 2 tell us). They took care of each other. They continued in fellowship.

They did this because they understood what we are studying here: they were the Church, and they were members together of Christ, and thus were members of one another individually (as Romans 12:4-5 literally says).

They knew they were together a Body. They knew they were a family, with the same Head, Christ Jesus. They knew, by divine appointment, they needed each other. They knew water was thicker than blood. Say what?

We've all heard many times the saying "blood is thicker than water," by which is meant that family should be preferred before anyone else. However, in Mark 3:31-35, the Word of God records:

> Then His brothers and His mother came, and standing outside they sent to Him, calling Him. And a multitude was sitting around Him; and they said to Him, "Look, Your mother and Your brothers are outside seeking You." But He answered them, saying, "Who is My mother, or My brothers?" And He looked around in a circle at those who sat about Him, and said, "Here are My mother and My brothers! "For whoever does the will of God is My brother and My sister and mother."

When you are baptized, and undergo that Covenant entrance ritual, it symbolizes the fact the Holy Spirit has placed you within the Body of Christ, and that your ultimate loyalty, your ultimate allegiance, is to the Lord Jesus, Who is the Head of the Body of Christ and of the Family of God. It makes you someone who is a part of a Colony, of a group, of a Body, of a Family, of a Liberating Army, who is a Weapon, and that loyalty to Christ transcends everything else. Our ultimate loyalty is to the Lord Jesus and His Body.

Seem a bit too radical for you, disciple? Let's look at Matthew 10:34-39:

> Do not think that I came to bring peace on earth. I did not come to bring peace but a sword. For I have come to '*set a man against his father, a daughter against her mother, and a daughter-in-law against her mother-in-law*'; and '*a man's enemies will be those of his own household.*' He who loves father or mother more than Me is not worthy of Me. And he who loves son or daughter more than Me is not worthy of Me. And he who does not take his cross and follow after Me is not worthy of Me. He who finds his life will lose it, and he who loses his life for My sake will find it. He who receives you receives Me, and he who receives Me receives Him who sent Me.

So, do we think the Lord Jesus is playing at these things? Do we not see He is deadly serious about following Him? He *demands* the absolute allegiance of His People, His Church. The water of Baptism divides the Church from Satan's dark anti-kingdom, and that division cuts across even our blood lines.

The Early Church understood this. How did they know this? They knew because they continued steadfastly together in the Apostles' Teaching. They were taught

God's Word, they saw themselves in its light, and they understood that their destiny lay together.

Now there are a lot of other Christians that many of us know and don't like (or don't like much, or that we think are beneath us, or are dorks, etc., etc.), but all of our destinies lie *together*. (Kind of a scary thought, until you consider the alternative…). This is a true saying: We will spend eternity together forever. Get used to the idea. There's no way out. We've got to learn to live together, because we are bound together, members of one another, forever. (The good news here is that all of us will be glorified and perfected, *cf.* 1 John 3:2-3; 1 Corinthians 15:47-57, and that this will fix us all, even the pride and self-centeredness which keep us from loving our brothers and sisters as we ought).

Eternity rules our destiny. You are going to live forever in this same colony of people, and this means not just the people in your congregation, or even just in your city, or even in your region, or the United States, or even in the world now, or even the Church in the Middle Ages, or the Old Testament, or the people we're studying in Acts chapter 2, but even all those as well in the future. We're all going to live together forever. Our colony, the Colony of Heaven, extends across all time and space, to be gathered together as we die until we are all assembled at Doomsday (though in worship, which transcends time and space, we are all gathered all at once into the Throne Room of God together as we are drawn in worship spiritually into the Presence of God, as Hebrews 12:22-24 tells us, as we'll see in a later chapter). All of us, together, forever, in the fellowship of the Undiluted Light of God. There is no way out of this for a Christian. This is your destiny. All of us are called to be a *fellowship* of believers.

John 17:20-26 tells us that Jesus said, in His Prayer in Gethsemane Garden,

"I do not pray for these alone, but also for those who will believe in Me through their word; that they all may be one, as You, Father, *are* in Me, and I in You; that they also may be one in Us, that the world may believe that You sent Me. And the glory which You gave Me I have given them, that they may be one just as We are one: I in them, and You in Me; that they may be made perfect in one, and that the world may know that You have sent Me, and have loved them as You have loved Me. Father, I desire that they also whom You gave Me may be with Me where I am, that they may behold My glory which You have given Me; for You loved Me before the foundation of the world. O righteous Father! The world has not known You, but I have known You; and these have known that You sent Me. And I have declared to them Your name, and will declare *it,* that the love with which You loved Me may be in them, and I in them."

Since Jesus prayed that the world would know the Father had sent Him, and has loved His People by their unity (verses 21 and 23), the opposite corollary comes into view: the world can draw the conclusion that the Father has *not* sent the Christ with Whom He is One, and that God does *not* love His People, and will *not* believe these things if the Church does not in their diversity display God's Unity, e.g., if the Church is not one in love, displaying the Pattern of the Life of the Holy Trinity and the Triune God's Love for humanity. Our unity and love demonstrate that God's Word is true. We think our squabbles are no big deal, but they are a *huge* deal, with unbelievably important implications.

This means that we can't be lazy, or prefer ourselves to someone else in the Church; if we're going to spend our eternity together, then we should work as hard as we can to help each other be the people that God wants us to be. Plus, we should let others help us, because we are going to be together forever.

3) Acts 2:42 goes on to list a third Defining Mark of the Church in which these believers continued steadfastly: The Breaking of Bread. This phrase means a couple of things. First, they ate together a lot. Whenever families or friends can, they get together and share a meal. This is true all over the world. Everyone likes to get together

and eat. This is the central action of joining together in fellowship.

Though this is true, however, this is not *primarily* what this Scriptural phrase means. In the Biblical Greek, this was a technical term (*te klasei tou artou*), which represented what we think of as the Lord's Supper, or the Eucharist, or Communion, the ritual liturgical meal that re-affirms our Covenant with God through Jesus Christ.

These people not only *ate* together, but they constantly *worshipped* together in the context of their meals (Agape Feasts, as they were called), during which they celebrated the liturgy, or ritual, of the Lord's Supper, just as the Old Covenant Jews before them had done in the Passover Meal. (Remember that Jesus instituted the Lord's Supper by adapting and changing the Passover Meal on the Thursday before His Crucifixion and Passion, *cf.* Matthew 17:14-30; Mark 14: 22-25; Luke 22:1-22). These Christians worshipped in their meals together because what they shared and continued in together was what we would call *sacramental life.*

You'll notice that right before this verse (in verse 41 of Acts 2) these 3000 people were *baptized*, which rite is the Covenant entrance ritual to the life of the Church, the *initiation* to the Church. Baptism is a Sacrament which shows that the one baptized is a part of the Church in the Life of God. It is to be a one-time, unrepeatable act (Ephesians 4:43).

The *other* Sacrament we're given is Communion, the Lord's Supper, which has to do with Covenant reaffirmation and the giving of grace which is in the Covenant for believers. The life of these Christians was characterized by observing the Sacraments, Sacramental worship, which is most important, as we'll see in pages to come. Thus, the third Mark is Sacramental Worship. They preached and taught and learned, continuing in the Apostolic Doctrine together in a life of committed fellowship, observing the Sacraments and worshipping together constantly.

4) Prayers. Acts 2:42 also says the believers continued steadfastly "in prayers" (or, more literally, "in the prayers," *kai tais proseuchais*, likely alluding to set, liturgical prayers, which Early Christian worship, like the Jewish Church before them, used constantly, both in public and private worship).

These people prayed a lot. Most Americans find this a difficult thing to understand. My father has a ministry in Hindustan, where, in places, 40% of Christian converts are martyred. Four people in ten. When these Indians convert, it's a risk: They are abandoned by their families, which entails a loss of caste and place in Hindu society, and they are frequently murdered for their faith. The Church in Acts (and for some 300 years afterwards) faced a similar situation both inside and outside of the Roman Empire. If you read past chapter 2 in Acts, you'll see the Christians faced what Indian converts in Hindustan (and in Muslim countries) face today. Prayer, in such a situation, becomes very important.

Prayer represents, on one hand, worship, and on the other, that those praying have *need* of God and His Aid. The Church in Acts *knew* they had need of God, but not only for protection. If you read the prayers of the Church recorded in Acts, you'll see they are not primarily prayers for protection, but are pleas for God to do what He purposes to do, showing His Glory, giving His Servants boldness to speak His Word, and to support the Church's witness with His Supernatural Power, so His Kingdom could advance and His Story, the Gospel, could spread (*cf.* Acts 4:24-31).

They were motivated to live their lives for a purpose greater than any other in their individual or corporate lives: to spread the Gospel and grow the Colony of Heaven, and thereby forward Christ's Glory on earth. This unified their lives and gave them an all-consuming purpose, throwing them together, because they understood they weren't just a bunch of individuals, but rather desperately needed each other and the Lord they served together.

It's harder to remember this presently in the United States, because there's not a great deal of persecution going on (some, but not much) *yet*. However, more persecution is likely coming, as our society progressively becomes more pagan. If the Church becomes what it is meant to be, our society will be renewed and reformed, especially since, when the Church is being all the things it should be (when it is being all the things it actually *is* in Christ), all the deep things humans seek are *in* the Church—love, acceptance, forgiveness, truth, community, healing, security, mystery, reason, etc. These are all in the Church, and when people see that in truth, they are drawn to all those things they need, which are all reflections of the Lord Who indwells the Church.

These are the Four Marks of the Church: (1) The Word of God, (2) Fellowship, (3) Sacramental Worship, and (4) Prayer. All four of these are absolutely essential to the well-being and freedom of the Church, your congregation, your family, your friends, and your own personal life, and through all of these, to the life of the world Jesus died to save, both now and to come.

These are the Marks of the Colony of Heaven. Because of that, these are also the Marks of a disciple of Jesus Christ: these Marks are what a disciple looks like, and the goal of all discipleship. By these Marks God will advance His Kingdom, bring His Glory more fully to the earth, draw people to the Faith, and be pleased Himself.

You'll note these Marks flow from what the Church is, from the modes of being of the Church we've seen. The steadfast continuance in the study and living out of the Word of God is what flows from and informs the Church as the Pillar and Ground of the Truth, since it teaches us, as fruit of discipleship, what truth is. It also helps the Church understand what we are as a Weapon, since it is the Word we know and live out which is the "Sword of the Spirit" (Ephesians 6:17), "living and powerful, and sharper than any two-edged sword, piercing even to the division of soul and spirit, and of joints and marrow, and is a discerner of the thoughts and intents of the heart" (Hebrews 4:12). The preaching, teaching, and living out of the Word by the Church, is what powers and models the freedom that the Church brings as a Liberating Force.

Steadfastly continuing in Fellowship is a natural by-product of the fact that in Christ we are His Body and a Family, flowing from the love from and toward the Lord and each other generated by the Romance of God's Love and Actions for us, His Bride.

Steadfastly continuing in Sacramental Worship is, of course, a function of the fact that the Church is a Temple, as is Prayer, though steadfastly continuing in Prayer is also a function of the Church as a Weapon (since our prayers move God to act, *cf.* Acts 12:1-25; Revelation 8:3-4), as a Liberating Force (since prayer does move God to act for His People), and as a Family (since we pray for those we love). All these aspects are tied together for the Church, the Colony of Heaven. You, personally, and we, as a people, will only fulfill our destiny and achieve what we were created to do by way of these seven Modes and four

Marks of being and action, so we should try to remember them.

When it's least expected, you're elected. Batter up. Only we, as the Church, can turn our society around. Ready or not, here it comes.

CHAPTER 3

GIFTS FOR THE BODY

So far in this study, we've seen the Seven Modes of the Church, the ways of being which characterize believers in the Lord Jesus (Romance, Family, Body, Temple, Pillar and Ground of Truth, Weapon, Liberating Force) as they inform and give rise to the Four Marks of the Church, the habitual actions which define those who are the Church (Study and living out of God's Word, Fellowship, Sacramental Worship, and Prayer).

To help us in being and doing these things, God has given the Church (every one of us) spiritual gifts. Paul the Apostle wrote to the Corinthian Church in 1 Corinthians 12:1, "Now concerning spiritual gifts, brethren, I do not want you to be ignorant," and neither do I, so let's look at what he had to say to these believers in this chapter, because what the Spirit says through Paul here is also about you and me:

There are diversities of gifts, but the same Spirit. There are differences of ministries, but the same Lord. And there are diversities of activities, but it is the same God who works all in all. But the manifestation of the Spirit is given to each one for the profit *of all:* for to one is given the word of wisdom through the Spirit, to another the word of knowledge through the same Spirit, to another faith by the same Spirit, to another gifts of healings by the same Spirit, to another the working of miracles, to another prophecy, to another discerning of spirits, to another *different* kinds of tongues, to another the interpretation of tongues. But one and the same Spirit works all these things, distributing to each one individually as He wills.

For as the body is one and has many members, but all the members of that one body, being many, are one body, so also *is* Christ. For by one Spirit we were all baptized into one body—whether Jews or Greeks, whether slaves or free—and have all been made to drink into one Spirit. For in fact the body is not one member but many. If the foot should say, "Because I am not a hand, I am not of the body," is it therefore not of the body? And if the ear should say, "Because I am not an eye, I am not of the body," is it therefore not of the body? If the whole body *were* an eye, where *would be* the hearing? If the whole *were* hearing, where *would be* the smelling? But now God has set the members, each one of them, in the body just as He pleased. And if they were all one member, where *would* the body *be?* But now indeed *there are* many members, yet one body. And the eye cannot say to the hand, "I have no need of you"; nor again the head to the feet, "I have no need of you." No, much rather, those members of the body which seem to be weaker are necessary. And those *members* of the body which we think to be less honorable, on these we bestow greater honor; and our unpresentable *parts* have greater modesty, but our presentable *parts* have no need. But God composed the body, having given greater honor to that *part* which lacks it, that there should be no schism in the body, but *that* the members should have the same care for one another. And if one member suffers, all the members suffer with *it;* or if one member is honored, all the members rejoice with *it.* Now you are the body of Christ, and members individually (1 Corinthians 12:4-27).

Let's break this down a bit, and see the meaning of these things more closely. Verses 4-6 of 1 Corinthians 12 read "There are diversities of gifts, but the same Spirit. There are differences of ministries, but the same Lord. And there are diversities of activities, but it is the same God who works all in all." These verses teach us that, although there are different gifts given out (there is diversity of gifts), these differing gifts are all given by the One Spirit of God, for a unified purpose: the many gifts serve the One Body of Christ in accomplishing the Unified Purposes of God. There is unity in diversity—many gifts, one Body.

We shouldn't be surprised at this, because the God Who made and redeemed us is a Triune God; He is a Trinity, One in His Essence or Being, but, at the same time, and just as much as He is One in His Essence, He also exists as Three Persons (and always has). God Himself is One and Many, Unified and Diversified; to see God is to see both Unity and Diversity all at the same time. The Church He has redeemed to reveal Himself through also reflects the Ways God is One and Many: we are diverse individuals with differing gifts (just as the Persons of the Trinity—Father, Son, and Spirit—are Diverse Persons with Differing Functions), but we are part of One Body of Christ with a unified destiny, calling, and purpose (just as the Persons of the Trinity are always Unified in Their Being and Purpose). Our differences are to be unified in our being and purpose, and our unity (as members of Christ and each other, as Romans 12:5 tells us) is to be supported and expressed through our various gifts and specialized ministries. If the Church does this correctly, it reveals in itself an image of the Triune God Who made and redeemed the Church.

Paul emphasizes unity here because there were members of the Corinthian congregation who were teaching that some members of the Church were superior to other members because their gifts were more important (in other words, that diversity was more important than unity), but Paul was showing that all the members of the Church (with their diverse gifts) are equally important to the mission and purposes of the Church. Both unity and diversity are to be seen as equally important, just as God's Essence and Persons are equally important.

This emphasis is carried on in verse 7: "But the manifestation of the Spirit is given to each one for the profit *of all.*" Our gifts are given to each of us (and you should also realize here that, if you are a Christian, you *have* been given a gift by the Holy Spirit) for the profit of everyone in the Church, *not* to glorify or promote oneself (which is what some of the Corinthian Christians were thinking). I don't get to just exercise my gift for myself; the aim is to *edify* (build up) others in the Church. We use our gifts to build up the *whole* Church, not just so me and Jesus can have our own thing going. Different gifts are designed to meet different needs (and rightfully so). The Gifts are given to meet needs; God is not a fool: He gives specific gifts to meet specific needs. The Church needs administrators as much as it needs teachers; we need faith as much as we need wisdom.

First Corinthians 12:8-10 gives us a list of gifts:

...for to one is given the word of wisdom through the Spirit, to another the word of knowledge through the same Spirit, to another faith by the same Spirit, to another gifts of healings by the same Spirit, to another the working of miracles, to another prophecy, to another discerning of spirits, to another *different* kinds of tongues, to another the interpretation of tongues.

This is not a complete list of the Gifts of the Spirit. It may contain the ones most evident in Corinth at the time (you'll note, for instance, the list in verse 28 of this passage in 1 Cor. 12 differs from the one in Romans 12:6-8). It does, however, (1) give the reader a sense of the sort of needs experienced by the members of the Church, (2) demonstrate that the Source of all the gifts is supernatural, (3) show that no one member of the Church possesses all the gifts, and that, thus, (4) we need each other, a point Paul drives home later in the passage.

Paul goes on in verse 11 to write, "But one and the same Spirit works all these things, distributing to each one individually as He wills." We don't get to decide what gift we get. The Spirit distributes individually as He wills. He decides, predicated on His Will for the Church, as a sovereign would. Even a Christian's legitimate desire for specific gifts (and there are situations where a congregation needs the exercise of a particular gift and no member there possesses that gift), as seen in verse 31 of this passage and in 1 Corinthians 14:39, must be submitted to the Will and Wisdom of the Holy Spirit Who Gives the gifts.

We should remember that birthday or Christmas gifts are *given*. We can either be content with a gift or not, but a gift is given by the grace and at the will of the giver, not the receiver.

The Lord gives by His Will because we frequently *want* not what we *need*, but simply what we want.

God is Smarter than to let us choose, with our limited understanding and perverse desires. We are gifted as we are to fulfill particular *needs*. You are gifted as you are for a purpose. It's no accident that you are where you are. You are needed, and your *gift* is needed where you are. Don't rob the Church of your gift.

"For as the body is one and has many members, but all the members of that one body, being many, are one body, so also *is* Christ." Verse 12 points out again that the many diversely-gifted members of the Body of Jesus are still one Body. This should be easy for us to grasp, since each of us have different members or parts of our individual bodies which, even though our body parts differ, are still all parts of our *one* body. Just so does Christ in His Body, and we should realize the Creator designed our physical bodies in part to reveal this very truth.

It gets weirder than that, though: The Church *is* one Church. The churches in India are still one Church. The million-plus-strong congregation in Seoul is still one Church. All the churches across the earth are still one Church. Not only that, but the congregation being addressed in 1 Corinthians in the first century is still one Church with us *now*. The Early, Medieval, and Reformation Churches? These are still one Church with us now. The believers who are not yet born? These also are one Church with us. The Church is one in Christ across space and time. We are members of them, and they are members of us, as Romans 12:5 tells us is true of all the members of Christ's Body.

The unity of the Church across time and space tells us your gifts have been given to you not just for the needs of the congregation you're currently serving, but also for the Church around the world and in the future (since you've been born only at the beginning of your lifetime, the Church in the past can't directly benefit from your gift, though you have already benefitted from the gifts of those who came before you...). The exercise of your gift in the congregation where you serve, in building up the members there, can easily affect the rest of the Church in our time, not only through those members giving money to help the Church elsewhere in its needs, but also by encouraging missionary efforts here and abroad, and, very importantly, by encouraging prayer for the Church across the globe, even in the future.

Likewise, the building up of the Body in our time will inexorably lead to conversions, the production of teaching and preaching resources to carry the Gospel into the future, the preservation of the nation by functioning as salt and light to arrest evil (Matthew 5:13-16), and the continuance of the worship of God and resultant sanctification of culture, all of which will provide a bridge to, and positive effect on, the Church which is yet to come.

Even beyond this, the Lord Who orders our lives and knows our futures has gifted us so that we can not only meet the needs of the part of the Church we are currently serving, but also for the needs of any congregation anywhere we'll be across our lives, since we are called at times to other places or parts of the Body. God has gifted you for all the places you'll be across the span of your life.

Then, in verse 13, Paul addresses the means by which we *become* members of Christ and of one another: "For by one Spirit we were all baptized into one body—whether Jews or Greeks, whether slaves or free—and have all been made to drink into one Spirit." All Christians have been baptized by the Spirit into Christ's One Body. Water Baptism signifies and seals the Baptism by the Holy Spirit which incorporates and places us into the Covenant People, the Church. Baptism has replaced circumcision as the sign of admission into the Church (Colossians 2:11-14; we no longer shed blood in the Covenant entrance rite because Jesus has once-and-for-all shed His Blood to buy us that privilege, as Hebrews 10:10 says), and the Eucharist or Lord's Supper signifies our continuing communion with Christ and His Church (1 Corinthians 10:16-17; 11:29).

Paul (in balanced Trinitarian fashion) switches back to diversity in unity in verse 14, as he has, as we've seen, been emphasizing unity in diversity in the preceding verses of the passage. At this point he begins to show that the Church's very diversity is inevitably engaged with its unity in Christ: "For in fact the body is not one member but many." The One Body of Christ has many members, but is still unified by the fact that these diverse members are all part of the same Body, and that is a necessary state if the Body is going to function as it should. The very diversity of the Body means that it is able, through the diverse gifts (and resultant functions) of those differing members, to accomplish all the things the Body must do if the Body is to obey the Will of the Head of the Body, the Lord Jesus.

All of God's Gifts are necessary to the Church's well-being and economy. To deny or question this is to question God's Authority and Sovereign Wisdom in giving each member of the Body their gift(s) (as verse 7 explicitly tells us God's Will is the origin of our gifts). This also means *every* Christian is *necessary* to the Church's well-being and mission. Your gift is desperately needed by the Church.

Of course, as is generally the case, privileges generally carry a measure of responsibility, and this one is a humdinger: If you don't use your gift as you should, it hurts us all, since the Church *needs* all its gifts. The downside of this great gifting from God is, if you blow it for *you*, you also blow it for *us*. Joshua 7 tells the story of Achan, who lost 36 lives for Israel because of his sin (which was hidden from the rest of the nation). We should strive not to be Achan to the Body of Christ.

In verses 15 and 16, Paul begins to flesh out the importance of the diversity of the gifts: "If the foot should say, "Because I am not a hand, I am not of the body," is it therefore not of the body? And if the ear should say,

"Because I am not an eye, I am not of the body," is it therefore not of the body?" One thing we should clearly take from this is that we'll only find our meaning (and the meaning of our gift) in the context of all the others. A finger lying by itself does nothing. Jesus designed life to be counter-intuitive (at least to our fallen self-orientation). To be great, you must be a servant (Mark 10:35–45). We are to serve to live, as Jesus did.

Some churches foolishly reject specific gifts (due to bad theology or fear). This *hurts* them (and the larger Church, as well, since, as we've seen, we are all connected). This is ecclesiastical suicide. Your gift, whatever it may be (and regardless of how men view it) is important and necessary to the Church.

Paul drives these points home in verse 17: "If the whole body *were* an eye, where *would be* the hearing? If the whole *were* hearing, where *would be* the smelling?" Each part of the Body desperately needs the others if it is to function. We *dare not* throw our gifts away, neither individually nor corporately. The American Church is currently in such bad shape partly because we've rejected gifts we really need. Reductionism is killing us.

God determines which gifts the Church (and each of us) needs: "But now God has set the members, each one of them, in the body just as He pleased. And if they were all one member, where *would* the body *be*? But now indeed *there are* many members, yet one body." Verses

18-20 not only attribute the setting of gifted members to the Providence and Wisdom of the Spirit, but also teach us here that to reject our gifts is to reject a part of our God-given purpose, what we were made for. God has set each member "just as He pleased;" if they *weren't* diverse and different, the Body could not function. You can't, as it were, pick your nose with no fingers. The diversity serves the unity, and vice-versa.

Verses 21-26 unpack that idea: "And the eye cannot say to the hand, "I have no need of you"; nor again the head to the feet, "I have no need of you." No, much rather, those members of the body which seem to be weaker are necessary. And those *members* of the body which we think to be less honorable, on these we bestow greater honor; and our unpresentable *parts* have greater modesty, but our presentable *parts* have no need. But God composed the body, having given greater honor to that *part* which lacks it, that there should be no schism in the body, but *that* the members should have the same care for one another. And if one member suffers, all the members suffer with *it;* or if one member is honored, all the members rejoice with *it.*"

To continue the theme, if you couldn't urinate or defecate, or digest food, or belch, you'd be in serious trouble physically. *All* of you, your *entire* body, would be very sick and eventually die. You can live without a tongue, or fingers, or with a disfigured face, but you cannot continue to live without a urinary or digestive tract. We give lots of attention to the parts of us that allow us to do these things, since, if they hurt or suffer, the whole body does.

Yet we think these parts (at least publicly) to be "less honorable," though we give them more attention and time. The Scripture here tells us that God has designed the body so we would give more attention to the necessary parts of the body which receive less honor precisely to teach us the same lesson about *His* Body, that the less noticeable or vaunted parts of the Body would necessarily be given the attention needed to promote unity, teach us the real value of *all* the gifts of the various members, and avoid "schism," which is to say, division in the Church. We are, despite our varied gifts and ministries within the Body, one united Body in Christ.

This is why, if one of the members suffer, we all suffer. This is also why, if one member is honored, we are all honored. If honor is to one member of the Body, all are honored, and we in truth share the honor of those members honored (this is why we love it when a Christian artist or politician is successful; they're part of us, and vice-versa). When someone admires the ministry of Billy Graham, they are also honoring his wife and family, the driver who takes him around, the staff member who books his engagements, and so forth. Billy Graham can't do his ministry alone; he is part of a larger entity that makes his ministry possible. When someone attends a service at a local congregation and very much appreciates it, he is also giving honor not only to the preacher and musicians, but to the janitorial staff who cleans the church, the altar guild who attends to the flowers, vestments, layout of the Table in the Lord's Supper, and to the volunteers who keep the grounds squared away, and even to the resident congregation who support all these things via prayer, service, and financial contribution.

As Alexandre Dumas long ago said of the Musketeers, "All for one, and one for all" is the actual truth concerning the Church. Thus you and I, regardless of our gifts and ministries, whether they are more noticed or publicly honored or are less so, are vital to the Church's well-being. We are needed, by the Wisdom of God, for His Body's purposes. We should all, in light of this, perhaps spread the honor around the Church with more deliberate appreciation.

Here in verse 27 is the kicker, the main point of this passage: "Now you are the body of Christ, and members individually." Just as the Persons of the Trinity cannot be separated from the Oneness of the Godhead, in the same way the Unity of God is always manifested in His Three Diverse Persons (a sort of metaphysical feedback loop). The Church is like that, as well, in ways; you help give the Church its meaning by your giftedness and calling, but you can only find your meaning in the Church, amidst all your sisters' and brothers' gifts and callings. There is a true saying that there is no lone ranger Christianity. God works with Covenanted peoples, with nations (and the Church *is* a nation, cf. 1 Peter 2:9), with tribes. You are, together, the Church, and individually are parts of the Church. You *are* the Church, but you are never the Church *alone*.

Paul also addressed the issue of our callings and gifts in Ephesians 4:7-16:

But to each one of us grace was given according to the measure of Christ's gift. Therefore He says:

"*When He ascended on high,*

He led captivity captive,

And gave gifts to men."

(Now this, *"He ascended"*—what does it mean but that He also first descended into the lower parts of the earth? He who descended is also the One who ascended far above all the heavens, that He might fill all things.) And He Himself gave some *to be* apostles, some prophets, some evangelists, and some pastors and teachers, or the equipping of the saints for the work of ministry, for the edifying of the body of Christ, till we all come to the unity of the faith and of the knowledge of the Son of God, to a perfect man, to the measure of the stature of the fullness of Christ; that we should no longer be children, tossed to and fro and carried about with every wind of doctrine, by the trickery of men, in the cunning craftiness of deceitful plotting, but, speaking the truth in love, may grow up in all things into Him who is the head—Christ— from whom the whole body, joined and knit together by what every joint supplies, according to the effective working by which every part does its share, causes growth of the body for the edifying of itself in love.

The very first line of this passage (verse 7) tells us that we have all been given grace by the Sovereign Measure of Jesus' Gift (reinforcing what Paul wrote in 1 Corinthians 12:11, as we've seen). What Jesus has given us by His Spirit, He gave with specific purpose in His Mind, which makes those gifts and callings vital and irreplaceable; all are needed.

After recounting what Christ did to win the ability to give those gifts and callings in verses 8 through 10 of Ephesians 4, Paul writes in verses 11-12: "And He Himself gave some *to be* apostles, some prophets, some evangelists, and some pastors and teachers, for the equipping of the saints for the work of ministry, for the edifying of the body of Christ..."

Here are listed various offices of ministry of the Church, followed by the reason Christ gave those offices to the Church: "for the equipping of the saints" (the Church) "for the work of ministry," which is to say, for service that leads to "the edifying (which means "building" or "building up") of the Body of Christ." For what is the Body of Christ to be equipped to be built up?

Verse 13: "till we all come to the unity of the faith and of the knowledge of the Son of God, to a perfect man, to the measure of the stature of the fullness of Christ." The

Body is to be built up until the Church is unified in faith and in the knowledge of Christ to perfection, "to the measure of the stature of the Fullness of Christ," e.g., until we're all we *can* be as a people in Christ, totally fulfilling His Purposes for us as His Church. Why?

Verses 14-15: "that we should no longer be children, tossed to and fro and carried about with every wind of doctrine, by the trickery of men, in the cunning craftiness of deceitful plotting, but, speaking the truth in love, may grow up in all things into Him who is the head—Christ..." so that we will become mature, unshakeable by bad beliefs or Satan's assaults on the Church, but, even in the face of such beliefs and assaults, speak the truth in love (*both*, not one or the other, as the modern Church is so likely to do, pitting truth against love and opting for one or the other, rather than doing both as Scripture demands). This building up of the Church is so we will "grow up in all things into Him who is the Head-Christ," and by so doing become all He intends for us to be in fulfilling His Goals and Desires for us, serving Him fully, just as our own bodies do us.

This is to be made possible by what is revealed in verse 16: "...from whom the whole body, joined and knit together by what every joint supplies, according to the effective working by which every part does its share, causes growth of the body for the edifying of itself in love."

This growth of the Body is to be brought about by every joint, every part, every member doing its share, supplying what it is meant to supply for the whole Church, causing growth by building up the Church in love by fulfilling its calling and using its gift to do so. Who you are, what you are, and what you have been given are vitally needed by the Church. Not just your congregation or youth group or denomination, but the *whole* Church *needs* you, as you *need* them.

Our gifts find their true and full meaning *only* in the context of the Body, the Church, since our gifts were given to us by God to be used in community with others, and are primarily given for the good of others. As we use them for the good of the others in the Church, we begin to see who we are and what our purpose and calling is in the Church community. We in this way begin to see our value and meaning as individuals as the other members respond to our own exercise of the specific gifts God has given us.

The other members of the Body, through their response and witness to the value of *our* gifts, help us to see how we contribute meaning and value individually to the whole Church as a community member. As our fellow members exercise *their* gifts toward us, they also help us to see who we are and what our value is altogether. We therefore need the Church community to discover our meaning and value to God's Kingdom.

Should the members (you and I) not supply what is needed, the Church will not fulfill its purpose in our time—the Church will fail to achieve its goal today. If the Church is to be and accomplish all it is to be and do, we must all work together for Christ's Common Good. No Christian is to live for himself, for we cannot live for ourselves without both destroying ourselves, wasting our life, *and* hurting the whole Church. We have been given gifts, but with those gifts comes *responsibility*. We've been given much, but as our Master has told us, to whom much is given, from him is much required (Luke 12:48). There are bad consequences if we do not fulfill our responsibility.

The Church is in trouble because Christians shirk their responsibility. The Church will fail in our generation if we fail to be who we are in truth. We stand or fall together, as a Body and People—there are no lone ranger Christians. As Saint John Calvin once wrote (quoting Saint Cyprian), "He who does not have the Church for his mother does not have God for his father." Be the Church.

Know the good. Love the good. Do the good.

Know the Lord. Love the Lord. Obey the Lord.

CHAPTER 4

HOW BIG IS THE GOSPEL?

The Church, the Colony of Heaven, is (1) Romance, (2) Family, (3) Body, (4) Temple, (5) Ground and Pillar of the Truth, (6) Weapon, and (7) Liberating Army. The Church is defined by Four Marks: (1) Studying and Teaching the Word, (2) Fellowship, (3) Sacramental Worship, and (4) Prayer, as we've seen. All these Modes of Being and Defining Marks are products of belief in, and the living out of the Gospel of Jesus Christ.

This is why the marching orders of the Church are summed up in the Great Commission of Matthew 28:18-20:

> And Jesus came and spoke to them, saying, "All authority has been given to Me in heaven and on earth. Go therefore and

make disciples of all the nations, baptizing them in the name of the Father and of the Son and of the Holy Spirit, teaching them to observe all things that I have commanded you; and lo, I am with you always, *even* to the end of the age." Amen.

Jesus said this to His disciples, and it came to represent the main thrust of their lives and work, as the Book of Acts and subsequent history show us.

The first thing Jesus says in this passage is that, "All authority has been given to Me in heaven and on earth." This is a very important statement, because it forms the backdrop of that which provides the power to accomplish the commands which follow it.

Jesus had, even prior to His Resurrection, told His disciples, "all things have been delivered to Me by My Father, and no one knows the Son except the Father. Nor does anyone know the Father except the Son, and the one to whom the Son wills to reveal Him" (Matthew 11:27) and Paul writes, "For this end [i.e., for this purpose] Christ died and rose and lived again, that He might be Lord of both the dead and the living" (Romans 7:9). Also, in Philippians 2:8-11, "And being found in appearance as a man, He humbled Himself and became obedient to the point of death, even the death of the cross. Therefore God also has highly exalted Him and given Him the name which is above every name, that at the name of Jesus every knee should bow, of those in heaven, and of those on earth, and of those under the earth, and that every tongue should confess that Jesus Christ is Lord, to the glory of God the Father."

Jesus' obedience unto death for our sins led to His Resurrection, His Victory over sin and death, and to His Ascension and Enthronement at the Right Hand of God in great power and majesty, far above all rule, authority, and power: 1 Corinthians 15:23-25: "But each one in his own order: Christ the firstfruits, afterward those who are Christ's at His coming. Then comes the end, when He delivers the kingdom to God the Father, when He puts an end to all rule and all authority and power. For He must reign till He has put all enemies under His feet."

Ephesians 1:20-22: "...which He worked in Christ when He raised Him from the dead and seated Him at His right hand in the heavenly places, far above all principality and power and might and dominion, and every name that is named, not only in this age but also in that which is to come. And He put all things under His feet, and gave Him to be head over all things to the church...."

First Peter 3:22, speaks of Christ, "Who has gone into heaven and is at the Right Hand of God, angels and authorities and powers having been made subject to Him."

The Lord Jesus' Exaltation to His Throne leads to a pouring out of His Grace (Acts 2:30-35). "Therefore, being a prophet, and knowing that God had sworn with an oath to him that of the fruit of his body, according to the flesh, He would raise up the Christ to sit on his throne, he, foreseeing this, spoke concerning the resurrection of the Christ, that His soul was not left in Hades, nor did His flesh see corruption. This Jesus God has raised up, of which we are all witnesses. Therefore being exalted to the right hand of God, and having received from the Father the promise of the Holy Spirit, He poured out this which you now see and hear. For David did not ascend into the heavens, but he says himself: 'The LORD said to my Lord, "Sit at My right hand, 'til I make Your enemies Your footstool."'" (*cf.,* Luke 24:44-49).

His Indwelling Presence in believers in a blessing resulting from His Exaltation in Glory (John 7:39; Galatians 4:6; 1 John 3:24; John 14:26; 16:7-14), and His first exercise toward us of His Royal Authority was the pouring out of His Spirit on His people. This was a celebration of His Coronation (His Crowning) by His giving gifts to His subjects, as a victorious king would upon his return in triumph after conquering his enemies, as Ephesians 4:7-12 tells us:

But to each one of us grace was given according to the measure of Christ's gift. Therefore He says: "When He ascended on high, He led captivity captive, and gave gifts to men." (Now this, "He ascended"—what does it mean but that He also first descended into the lower parts of the earth? He who descended is also the One who ascended far above all the heavens, that He might fill all things.) And He Himself gave some to be apostles, some prophets, some evangelists, and some pastors and teachers, for the equipping of the saints for the work of ministry, for the edifying of the body of Christ.

Those gifts God has given the Church? They came as the celebratory spoils of Jesus' having conquering death and Satan.

Not only does Jesus give the Church gifts, but His Enthronement promises His Royally Divine Intercession and Help for His people, as Romans 8:34 tells us: "Who is he who condemns? It is Christ who died, and furthermore is also risen, who is even at the right hand of God, who also makes intercession for us."

In Acts 5:31, Peter preaches Jesus as the Exalted Prince and Savior. God has *already* put all things under Christ's Feet (as the Greek shows in Ephesians 1:22: "And He put all things under His Feet, and gave Him to be Head over all things to the Church") and given Him a Name and Title higher than all others (ditto for the aorist past tense in the Greek in Philippians 2:9) at His Resurrection, Ascension, and Enthronement. This means that Jesus is ruling *now*, as Revelation 1:5 tells us: "and from Jesus Christ, the faithful witness, the firstborn from the dead, and *the ruler over the kings of the earth*." (my emphasis).

Why am I telling you all this data? What has it to do with you, especially in the context of the Great Commission? Well, Revelation 1:6 goes on to teach us that, not only has Jesus loved us and washed us from our sins in His own Blood (as vs. 5 told us), but "...has made us kings and priests to His God and Father, to Him be Glory and Dominion forever and ever. Amen."

Understand this—this is *most* incredible: Christians *now* rule and reign with Christ in the world.

Don't believe it? Let's look at a few passages. Ephesians 1:20-23 says:

> ...which He worked in Christ when He raised Him from the dead and seated Him at His right hand in the heavenly places, far above all principality and power and might and dominion, and every name that is named, not only in this age but also in that which is to come. And He put all things under His feet, and gave Him to be head over all things to the church which is His body; the fullness of Him who fills all in all.

This takes on greater meaning for us because "...when we were dead in trespasses, (He) made us alive together with Christ (by grace you have been saved), and raised us up together, and made us sit together in heavenly places in Christ Jesus" (Ephesians 2:5-6).

We are, in God's Eyes, seated with Jesus in heavenly places, i.e., in regal, ruling position. Still don't buy it?

Look at Romans 5:17: "For if by the one man's offence death reigned through the one, much more those who receive abundance of grace and of the gift of righteousness [e.g., us, the saved] *will reign in life through the One, Jesus Christ)."* (my emphasis). Pretty straight forward here. And 2 Timothy 2:12: "If we endure, we shall also reign with Him". Our true status, as God sees it, is shown in 1 Corinthians 3:21-23: "Therefore let no one boast in men. For *all things are yours*: whether Paul or Apollos or Cephas, or the world or life or death. Or things *present* or things to come–*all are yours*. And you are Christ's, and Christ is God's" (my emphasis).

We are *now* seated with Christ, with His Authority and Power, where He waits at this moment until the defeat of all His enemies takes place under His Glorious Reign of Grace, as Paul teaches in 1 Corinthians 15:23-28:

> But each one in his own order: Christ the firstfruits, afterward those who are Christ's at His coming. Then comes the end, when He delivers the kingdom to God the Father, when He puts an end to all rule and all authority and power. For He must reign till He has put all enemies under His feet. The last enemy that will be destroyed is death. For "He has put all things under His feet." But when He says "all things are put under Him," it is evident that He who put all things under Him is excepted. Now when all things are made subject to Him, then the Son Himself will also be subject to Him who put all things under Him, that God may be all in all.

And Hebrews 10:12-13 also teaches this: "But this Man, after He had offered one sacrifice for sins forever, sat down at the right hand of God, from that time waiting till His enemies are made His footstool." So, you see why it is that the statement in Matthew 28:18 (And Jesus came and spoke to them, saying, "All authority has been given to Me in heaven and on earth") is so important: Christ not only has all authority in heaven and on earth, and thus the Right and Power to send us out to succeed in His Name, but has given us derivatively His Power and Authority as well. As Jesus said, "…you shall receive power when the Holy Spirit has come upon you; and you shall be witnesses to Me in Jerusalem, and in all Judea and Samaria, and to the end of the earth" (Acts 1:8).

Therefore, with the very Power and Authority of Christ Himself, we are commanded to "Go therefore [the "therefore" refers to Christ's Authority in all things] and make disciples of all the nations…" Jesus commands us to go, and this implies that the Church, as a group, is to actively and aggressively endeavor to win the lost of the world, not only just in Jerusalem, but also in Judea, Samaria, and to the end of the earth. The pattern of our evangelism is to start at home and move outward until all the world nations are discipled.

The word translated as "Go" in Matthew 28:19 is the Greek word *poreuthentes*, which literally would be rendered "going", meaning something like "to go on one's way, to proceed from one place to another (from *poros*, a passage, a ford, English pore)" (W.E. Vine's *Expository Dictionary of New Testament Words;* p. 156, p. 2), and would carry for us this meaning in this context: "*As you are going.*" This implies we should be evangelizing wherever and whenever we go and that one of the meanings of our going anywhere at *all* should be to carry the Gospel to others.

It goes without saying, but I'll say it anyway, the Gospel we are to carry and preach to others is that Christ has come to pay the penalty for our sins by the shedding of His Blood in Sacrifice of Himself to Himself to satisfy His Own Holy and Righteous Justice (Acts 2:38; etc.). As Luke 24:46-48 says "…Thus it is written, and thus it was necessary for the Christ to suffer and to rise from the dead the third day, and that repentance and remission of sins should be preached in His name to all nations, beginning at Jerusalem. And you are witnesses of those things." This is the Gospel in a nutshell, a Gospel of salvation by God's Grace alone, not by any work we can do (Ephesians 2:8-10: For by grace you have been saved through faith, and that not of yourselves; it is the gift of God, not of works, lest anyone should boast. For we are His workmanship, created in Christ Jesus for good works, which God prepared beforehand that we should walk in them). This we are to preach *as we go.*

The Church is commanded to *baptize* its disciples (v.19). Surely this implies that they be admitted, recognized, loved and accepted by His Church. We are not to win them and then forget them; rather, we are to win them and establish them in the faith. Thus Paul did not merely preach the saving gospel; he instructed them, cared for them, and visited and re-visited them again and again. He admonished and encouraged them to obey the Lord in their service to Him and in their spiritual growth (Acts 15:36: Then after some days Paul said to Barnabas, "Let us now go back and visit our brethren in every city where we have preached the word of the Lord, and see how they are doing."). (Porter L. Barrington's note on Matthew 28:16-20, note 38, point (2), in *The Christian Life Edition of The New King James Version of the Holy Bible*, p. 892).

The activities of those baptized into Christ's Body in the Apostolic Church are shown in Acts 2:41-47 (Then those who gladly received his word were baptized; and that day about three thousand souls were added to them. And they continued steadfastly in the apostles' doctrine and fellowship, in the breaking of bread, and in prayers. Then fear came upon every soul, and many wonders and signs were done through the apostles. Now all who believed were together, and had all things in common, and sold their possessions and goods, and divided them among all, as anyone had need. So continuing daily with one accord in the temple, and breaking bread from house to house, they ate their food with gladness and simplicity of heart, praising God and having favor with all the people. And the Lord added to the church daily those who were being saved), where they become part of the corporate Church's doctrine and fellowship, sacraments and prayers (verse 42), even to the point of helping support one another financially (verses 44-45). They were baptized into a *way of life.*

This description of Christianity as a way of life (or a worldview as some people say) is very important, especially since this is not generally considered to be true of Christianity today in the Western World. Christianity is instead generally seen as a private, individual, inward experience rather than as a cohesive, coherent, interconnected, corporate way of life with other Christians together as a body, a corporate entity. This is very important because the failure of the Church in America and the West to recognize that Christianity is to be a total way of life has meant that both Communism and Islam, both of whom claim to have comprehensive views of life, have been an answer to their adherents because they *seem* to have an answer for *all* of life, while Christianity *seems not to,* because Christians have not represented or lived out their Faith in such a way as to let pagans know and see that Christianity *is* the only system that has answers for *all* of life. Many of you have seen how people in your schools, jobs, your acquaintances, etc., have rejected Christianity, thinking it inferior because they believe it shallow, narrow, and inadequate to meet all of life's challenges.

This is the context for my question, "How big is the Gospel?" Matthew 28:18-20 answers that question clearly. Verse 19 commands us to "make disciples of all nations". Most of us have been taught (or have assumed) that this means *only* that we are to make disciples *from* every nation (and it does mean this, but not *only* this), but in Greek this phrase "*matheteusate panta ta ethne*" literally means, "ya'll disciple the *nations,*" whole cultures, people, tribes (*ethne* is the word our English word *ethnic* comes from) — we are to disciple not just individuals, but whole peoples, cultures, *nations,* teaching them to "observe all things" (verse 20) Christ has commanded, thus renewing not only individuals, but their families, government , schools, laws, arts, marketplaces, etc.; e.g., their whole *nations.* This is the true scope of the Gospel, the answer to how big the Gospel is: big enough to embrace and change the entire *world.* Big enough for you? Second Corinthians 10:5 commands that we should be "casting down arguments and every high thing that exalts itself against the knowledge of God, bringing every thought into captivity to the obedience of Christ," so that even down to "every thought" is brought captive to Christ with the resultant discipling of the nations in *everything* Christ has commanded.

We've already seen that *all* forms of authority belong to Jesus, and through Him, under His Command, to us, since His Authority is over every realm, whether individual, inter-personal, familial, ecclesiastical, societal, political, economic, legal, artistic, scientific, etc.,—*all* areas. He is the "Ruler of the kings of the earth" (Revelation 1:5), and has a Name above all others (Philippians 2:10), and on the basis of that all-encompassing Authority, we are to urge repentance in each area of life so that a change of external behavior by being transformed by God instead of conformity to this world-system will be brought forth, such as that described in Romans 12:2: "Do not conform any longer to the pattern of this world, but be transformed by the renewing of your mind. Then you will be able to test and approve what God's will is—his good, pleasing and perfect will."

These changes are things even like caring for the poor (Luke 3:11), and being upright government officials (Luke 3:12-14), changes to affect us down to the taking of every last *thought* captive to Christ (2 Corinthians 10:4-5), doing *everything* to God's Glory, as 1 Corinthians 10:31 instructs: "Therefore, whether you eat or drink, or whatever you do, do all to the glory of God." We will, after all, give an account for everything we do and say to God (Matthew 12:36: "But I say to you that for every idle word men may speak, they will give account of it in the day of judgment;" Romans 14:12: "So then each of us shall give account of himself to God").

This can and does happen; it *works*. In Acts 19:11-41, we are told by Luke that the preaching of the Gospel was so powerful in Ephesus that people burned their expensive and revered magic books, and riots ensued led by idol makers for fear that their whole society would be out of work because of all the conversion in their city to Christ. In Acts 17:6, we are told the Christians were accused of being those who "turned the world upside-down," as they called on "all men everywhere to repent." Would that Christianity were thought of that way in our nation today. It can be, *if* we are faithful and obedient.

This is what the preaching of Christ's Gospel is to produce: complete societal change fueled by the Holy Spirit's Work of Sanctification in every area of regenerate man's lives. This is why the Old Testament prophets saw *all* the world at the preaching to Mount Zion (Isaiah 2:1-4; Micah 4:1-3). The result of the Gospel is to be Christians living and acting out in every area of life their faith with *all* of their bodies, souls, minds, and strength (Mark 12:30). Christ died to bring men *and* the world-system to salvation (John 1:29; 3:17; 1 John 2:2), and to redeem mankind (1 Timothy 2:6).

So, we are to go forth to conquer the world by His Gospel armed with His Authority (Matthew 28:18),

Presence (verse 20), and Command (verse 19), knowing that apart from Him we can do nothing (John 15:5), but in Christ we can do all things (Philippians 4:13, 19; Matthew 17:20). We must remember that the Gospel is the "Power of God unto salvation" (Romans 1:16; 1 Corinthians 1:24; 2:4; 1 Thessalonians 1:5), and we can expect God to empower His Gospel to accomplish His Purposes, since His Word *will* accomplish what He pleases (Isaiah 55:11).

You see the scope, the challenges, the opportunity, and privilege to take part in changing our world for Christ. Should being thought ridiculous or being embarrassed keep you from sharing and living out the Gospel to your neighbor? Matthew 22:39 teaches us that we must love our neighbor as ourselves, and Matthew 7:12 and Luke 6:31 teach us to do unto others as we would have them do unto us—the Golden Rule. To love our neighbors, we must tell and live out the Gospel to them. We're glad someone did this for us; now we must do it for others.

The most important thing, though, is to please Christ. If we love Him, we will keep His Commandments, since John 14:23-24 tells us: "Jesus answered and said to him, 'If anyone loves Me, he will keep My word; and My Father will love him, and We will come to him and make Our home with him. He who does not love Me does not keep My words; and the word which you hear is not Mine but the Father's Who sent Me." Do we love Him? It's not enough to simply feel an emotional attachment to Him. Love always results in actions which show that love is real. Love is primarily about ethics, not emotion. Will we obey His Commands, by preaching and living out His gospel? Will we, will *you*, change the world for Him?

CHAPTER 5

HOW DO WE FIGHT?

We've seen in the last chapter that one of the major tasks and privileges of the Church is to fulfill the Great Commission, a task that is much broader and all-encompassing than evangelism is normally conceived to be. Of the seven modes of the Church we've reviewed (Romance, Body, Family, Temple, Pillar and Ground of the Truth, Weapon, and Liberating Army), though *all* of these modes are impacted and partially fulfilled by the Great Commission's enactment (and all of the modes of the Church interpenetrate and inform one another), several of them are specifically embodied in Biblical Evangelism. The three most pertinent modes involved are Weapon, Liberating Army, and Pillar and Ground of the Truth.

Let's look first at the Pillar and Ground of the Truth, the phrase used by the Apostle Paul in 1 Timothy 3:15 to describe the Church, though some commentators and translators think it refers to the God of the Church, since the verse itself says, "the House of God, which is the Church of God, the Pillar and Ground of the Truth." If indeed the phrase "Ground and Pillar of the Truth" refers to God, His Church is still the community which alone in the world specifically is called to proclaim, teach, and live out, as the Family, Body, and Spirit-inhabited Temple of God, the Word of God. The Church *is* the Ground, the field of teaching and living, and thus the support of that teaching and living out, of God's Word.

How does this intersect with the Great Commission, you ask? Well, in Matthew 18: 19-20, we are commanded to "make disciples of all the nations...teaching them to observe (*keep* or *obey*) all that I have commanded you," thus, *all* the things Jesus has commanded. How do we know all that the Lord has commanded us? Second Timothy 3: 16-17 gives us the answer to that question:

> All Scripture is given by inspiration of God, and is profitable for doctrine, for reproof, for correction, for instruction in righteousness, that the man of God may be complete, thoroughly equipped for every good work.

Second Peter 1: 20 also speaks of Scripture as coming about not by "the will of man," but as the result of "holy men" speaking "as they were moved by the Holy Spirit."

The reason these passages help answer this question is that the Bible identifies the Holy Spirit as "the Spirit of Jesus Christ" in Philippians 1:19, which should not surprise us, since Christ Jesus is the Incarnate Second Person of the Trinity, Whose Divine and Human Natures are joined in One Person, so that not only does His Divinity share the Divine Substance with the Holy Spirit, but His Humanity is indwelt by that same Spirit. The Spirit is the One Who created the Human Nature in the Virgin Mary to Which the Divine Son would be joined to form the One Person of Jesus (Matthew 1:18), Who descended as a Dove on Jesus at His Baptism (Matthew 3:16), led Jesus to the Temple to be questioned by the teachers (Luke 2:27), in Whose Power Jesus ministered (Luke 4:14), and anointed Him (Acts 10:38). It's easy to see why the Scriptures (which the Holy Spirit inspired) refer to Him as the Spirit of Jesus. Since the Spirit is the One (as 2 Timothy 3:16 and 2 Peter 1:21 both teach) Who has inspired the Bible, and since He is the Spirit of Jesus, we know that the *entire* Bible, both Old and New Testaments, comprise all the things Christ has commanded us.

Though this at first may seem overwhelming, this fact is actually very helpful to us in obeying the Great Commission Christ has given us, since, if that were not so, we'd have much less information to tell us how to change the world by discipling the nations to obey all the things Jesus has commanded us.

Make no mistake about this, Scripture is intended to be a blueprint for our lives. As the Word of God tells us in 2 Timothy 3:16-17, the Scripture "is profitable for doctrine, for reproof, for correction, for instruction in righteousness, that the man of God may be complete, thoroughly equipped for every good work." This is a massively broad spectrum of possibilities: "every good work" includes every category of everything a Christian may be called to do in his or her life, for instance, a calling to politics, or art, or education, or being a mechanic, or a homemaker, or a minister, or a judge, or a soldier, etc. Scripture addresses all these areas by principle, precept, or example (and of every other area of life, as well).

The Spirit Who has empowered the creation of all these vocations and of every possibility of life, and given them their meanings, has also given us infallible guidance as to how we should live according to His Standards in all these arenas, which also providentially provides guidance as to the standards and criteria for discipling all the nations, as Jesus commanded us to do. He always provides the power and the means for what He commands, and in Scripture He gives us a map, a blueprint for how our lives, individually and collectively, are to be lived to His Glory.

As Isaiah 8:20 tells us, "To the law and to the testimony! If they do not speak according to this word, it is because there is no light in them." Illuminating light comes only from the Spirit of God Who has inspired the written Word of God, and from nowhere else, and any interpretation of the reality the Lord has made that does not agree with the teaching of the Bible is from the dark angel. See what is written in 1 Corinthians 2:9:

> But as it is written: "Eye has not seen, nor ear heard, nor have entered into the heart of man the things which God has prepared for those who love Him." But God has revealed them to us through His Spirit. For the Spirit searches all things, yes, the deep things of God. For what man knows the things of a man except the spirit of the man which is in him? Even so no one knows the things of God except the Spirit of God. Now we have received, not the spirit of the world, but the Spirit who is from God, that we might know the things that have been freely given to us by God. These things we also speak, not in words which man's wisdom teaches but which the Holy Spirit teaches, comparing spiritual things with spiritual. But the natural man does not receive the things of the Spirit of God, for they are foolishness to him; nor can he know them, because they are spiritually discerned. But he who is spiritual judges all things, yet he himself is rightly judged by no one. For "who has known the mind of the LORD that he may instruct Him?" But we have the mind of Christ.

Verses 9-11 tell us the Spirit knows the Depths of the Triune God as men know their own spirits. Verse 12 then tells us that we believers have been given the Spirit so we can *know* those truths which the Spirit reveals about God. Verse 13 teaches us that those Deep Things of God are revealed by the Spirit to apostles such as Paul who have taught them (and, indeed, this passage in First Corinthians 2 is a prime example of what Paul is claiming here), showing us also that these Deep Things of God have been transferred to Scripture, the repository of teaching given by the Spirit to the Biblical authors (Whom 1 Peter 1: 20-21 tells us is the ultimate origin of the Scriptures). Verses 14-15 teach us it is the Same Spirit Who inspired the Scriptures Who illumines them to us, since only the Spirit can give understanding to His Word. Finally, in this passage, verse 16 informs us these things illumined for us are the Very Wisdom of God, the "Mind of Christ."

The Spirit Who has created all things and inspired the writing of the Scriptures inhabits us (as the Temple of The Lord) and illumines us, giving us the Mind of Christ (as His Body), causing us to understand the light and wisdom in His Word, and empowering us to enact it, thus teaching us all the things Christ has commanded, so that we can obey His Great Commission and disciple all nations to do these things. It is only the Holy Spirit-inhabited Church which possesses the Mind of Christ, and is illuminated and empowered by Christ's Spirit to teach and live out the fullness of Scripture. This is why we, the Church of Jesus Christ, are in the Fallen world, the only Pillar and Ground of the Truth, where the Lord is to be revealed in

His Unique Fullness as the Redeemer of men and nations. This is an unbelievably great privilege and responsibility for the Church, for us who are God's Family. This is why we must learn and love God's Word, our blueprint and marching orders for the liberation of the world.

It is therefore a great tragedy that we know so little of our blueprint and battle plan. We know hundreds of song-lyrics, the names and statistics of athletes going back for years, the characters and story lines of soap operas going back decades, beaucoup lines from movies, the mileage and performances of any number of automobiles, the intricacies of our jobs, and so forth, yet we don't even know the fifteen verses of 3 John, the thirteen verses of 2 John, or the twenty-five verses of Jude, despite the fact that it is the Scriptures which contain the Word of God by which we know how to live and be free. That we know and spend our time learning so many things, but don't know the Bible is tantamount to spiritual suicide. We need to realize what is most important, and spend our lives on what truly matters.

It is this knowledge of God's Word which gives us our strategy and tactics as a Liberating Army, and tells us what our weapons, our tools of liberation, are. Yet such knowledge, without the power to utilize these things, would prove ultimately futile. This is not, however, the situation of the Church.

As we saw in the last chapter, we Christians are seated in the Ascended, Ruling Christ in Whom is all Authority in Heaven and on Earth (Ephesians 2:4-7; Colossians 2:9-10) and share, derivatively, His Authority. We have received Power from the Indwelling Holy Spirit (Acts 1:8) and are to do the same Works that Jesus did, as John 14:12 tells us:

> Most assuredly, I say to you, he who believes in Me, the works that I do he will do also; and greater works than these he will do, because I go to My Father.

One of the Primary Works Jesus did is laid out in 1 John 3:8: "For this purpose the Son of God was manifested, that He might destroy the works of the devil."

Because we share in Jesus' Authority, He Who has defeated Satan and His Kingdom and now rules over them (Colossians 2:19-20; Ephesians 1:20-23), we have also been given authority over Satan's evil world-system. In Luke 10:19-20 Jesus tells us:

> Behold, I have given you authority to tread on serpents and scorpions, and over all the power of the enemy, and nothing shall hurt you. Nevertheless do not rejoice in this, that the spirits are subject to you, but rather rejoice because your names are written in heaven.

Our authority is based on the fact that our names are written in Heaven (e.g., that we are positioned in Christ), which is why we are to rejoice in that reality (along with our eternal salvation and all our other benefits in Him), but we nonetheless should not lose sight of the truth that, because of our membership in His Body, we *do* possess authority over "all the power of the enemy," and are therefore safe from the enemy's attacks.

Now, our possession of this authority is not simply to be thought of as defensive (though it *is* that, as well), such as you see at times in horror films, but is to be understood in the context of the events recounted in Luke 10, where the seventy disciples have just returned from being sent out to preach about Christ and heal, etc., in His Name. On their return, the Seventy rejoiced, telling Jesus, "Lord, even the demons are subject to us in Your Name" (Luke 10:17). Their comment is made in the context of aggressive assault on Satan's kingdom, as those who are coming to faith are being freed from the Devil and those who are demonized are reacting and attempting to interfere with the Work of God through the Disciples. The Seventy have asserted authority over the demons in Jesus' Name, and the demons are forced to obey. The context is spiritual warfare, the liberation of people from Satan's power by the Authority of Jesus' Name, one of the Great Weapons vouchsafed to the Church of Christ.

This, of course, is not the only instance of the freeing of demonized individuals in the New Testament. Jesus repeatedly asserted His Authority over demons, as in Matthew 4:24; 8:16, 28-34; 12:22; 15:22-28; 17:15-21(only a partial list), and His Disciples, as we've seen, did the same in His Name, as they are recorded doing also in Mark 16:12-13; Acts 5:16; Acts 16:16-18, etc. We are called, as believers, to make war on Satan's kingdom, primarily through preaching the Gospel, but such an assault on those held captive by the devil (which is the situation of *all* unbelievers, as Ephesians 2:1-3 lays out) generally elicits Satan's fierce resistance and counterattacks, requiring that we be able to exercise authority over his evil spirits. An example of this is clearly laid out in Acts 13:5-12, which recounts the resistance of the Jewish sorcerer Elymas Bar-Jesus, who was attached to the court of the Roman Proconsul of Paphos, and who sought to discredit Paul's preaching of the Gospel to the Proconsul. Paul pronounced Divine Judgment on Elymas, and the Lord blinded him, resulting in the Proconsul's faith and repentance.

Ephesians 6:10-18 describes our situation as the Weapon and Liberating Army of Christ:

> Finally, my brethren, be strong in the Lord and in the strength of his might. Put on the whole armor of God, that you may be able to stand against the wiles of the devil. For we do not wrestle against flesh and blood, but against principalities, against powers, against the rulers of the darkness of this age,

against spiritual hosts of wickedness in the heavenly places. Therefore take up the whole armor of God, that you may be able to withstand in the evil day, and having done all, to stand. Stand therefore, having girded your waist with truth, having put on the breastplate of righteousness, and having shod your feet with the preparation of the gospel of peace; above all, taking the shield of faith with which you will be able to quench all the fiery darts of the wicked one. And take the helmet of salvation, and the sword of the Spirit, which is the Word of God; praying always with all prayer and supplication in the Spirit, being watchful to this end with all perseverance and supplication for all the saints.

We can see several things clearly from this passage. We are to be strong in the strength of God's Might, depending on Him in all that He is and all He has given us, such as the Armor of God, each piece of which is vitally important if we are to be able to stand against Satan's stratagems. You'll note that most of these items are defensive items; only two of them are overtly aggressive, and only one is clearly a weapon "the Sword of the Spirit, which is the Word of God," the same Sword which is described in Hebrews 4:12: "For the Word of God is living and powerful, and sharper than any two-edged sword, piercing even to the division of soul and spirit, and of joints and marrow, and is a discerner of the thoughts and intents of the heart." A most powerful weapon.

Yet even though this is true (and you'll note there is no real protection for the wearer's back; there is to be no retreat), nonetheless, when this armor is donned, the wearer becomes *himself* the weapon—when we wear this armor, *we* are the Weapon, with the Authority of Christ, His Word, His Name, and the Empowerment of the Indwelling Spirit, a veritable nightmare in Satan's eyes, as the Weapon that can be used of God to free the devil's captives. As all the Church together, we are a Liberating Army.

And we *are* at war. Not with "flesh and blood, but against principalities, against powers, against the rulers of the darkness of this age, against spiritual forces in high places," as verse 12 here tells us. We are to advance in the Power of the Spirit, and "though we walk in the flesh, we do not war according to the flesh. For the weapons of our warfare are not carnal but mighty in God for pulling down strongholds, casting down arguments and every high thing that exalts itself against the knowledge of God, bringing every thought into captivity to the obedience of Christ" (1 Corinthians 10:3-5). Our weapons are *mighty* in God. We have been given the authority from Christ with an attendant promise: "Therefore submit to God. Resist the devil and he will flee from you" (James 4:7).

Most of us are not used to thinking of ourselves as weapons, or as locked in lifelong struggle with a powerful supernatural enemy, and many are afraid of becoming suddenly aware of the fact that they *are* inevitably locked in such a conflict. We, however, should remember all the things the Lord has given us to equip us to allow us to have victory over the devil. He Himself has said to us, "In the world you will have tribulation; but be of good cheer, I have overcome the world-system" (John 16:33), and "Do not fear, little flock, for it is your Father's good pleasure to give you the kingdom" (Luke 12:36). We are in Him, and He has overcome Satan's world-system, and shared His Power with us, that we might follow Him into battle.

The warfare passage in Ephesians 6 ends with an admonition to be "praying always with all prayer and supplication in the Spirit, being watchful to this end with all perseverance and supplication for all the saints," (verse 18). The "end" in question here is the struggle against Satan and his minions, and Scripture urges that prayer and supplication in the Spirit be constantly made for the army of saints, the Weapon of God, His Liberating Force.

Prayer itself is a powerful weapon in the mouths and hearts of the Church, even though it may not at first seem like it. Consider what the earliest Church in Jerusalem in the days after the Descent of the Spirit at Pentecost did following the release of Peter and John, who had been arrested for the healing of a man lame from birth which had led to many believing in Jesus (recounted in Acts 3 - 4:1-22).

And being let go, they went to their own companions and reported all that the chief priests and elders had said to them. So when they heard that, they raised their voice to God with one accord and said: "Lord, You are God, who made heaven and earth and the sea, and all that is in them, who by the mouth of Your servant David have said: 'Why did the nations rage, And the people plot vain things? The kings of the earth took their stand, And the rulers were gathered together Against the LORD and against His Christ.' For truly against Your holy Servant Jesus, whom You anointed, both Herod and Pontius Pilate, with the Gentiles and the people of Israel, were gathered together to do whatever Your hand and Your purpose determined before to be done. Now, Lord, look on their threats, and grant to Your servant that with all boldness they may speak Your Word, by stretching out Your hand to heal, and that signs and wonders may be done through the name of Your holy Servant Jesus." And when they had prayed, the place where they were assembled together was shaken; and they were all filled with the Holy Spirit, and they spoke the Word of God with boldness (Acts 4:23-31).

You'll note that, in response to the persecution of the Church, the Christians prayed together, and asked the Lord to respond in terms of identifying their situation with His Word (in this case, the quoting of Psalm 2), a passage wherein the Lord and His Messiah act in judgment against the enemies of the Messiah, as the Church essentially invoked God's Action against His enemies in terms of

His Word. As we've seen, the Scriptures *themselves* are a weapon, the Sword of the Spirit (Ephesians 6:17), and the Church uses it here in prayer, as we should.

Not only is the situation placed in the Hands of the Lord to be judged as He sees fit, but the gathered worshippers specifically ask God to answer the persecution by empowering them to preach the Gospel with both boldness and accompanying miraculous signs. God's response was to shake the building, fill the Church with the Empowering Spirit, and anoint them to preach with boldness, as verse 31 and the following chapters of Acts clearly demonstrate.

While this is perhaps not what we would expect from a weapon, the fact of the matter is that, even aside from the Church's invocation of God's Word, the anointing of God by His Spirit to empower and accompany with miracles the preaching of the believers was an overt act of war against Satan's kingdom by the Lord, as His Empowerment of His Church made them even more efficient weapons than they had been before. It was precisely the preaching of the Gospel with such power that would eventually bring about the conversion of the Roman Empire. Prayer is itself a weapon.

At times, however, prayer is more directly what we might think of as an assault. Consider Revelation 8:2-5:

And I saw the seven angels who stand before God, and to them were given seven trumpets. Then another angel, having a golden censer, came and stood at the altar. He was given much incense, that he should offer it with the prayers of all the saints upon the golden altar which was before the throne. And the smoke of the incense, with the prayers of the saints, ascended before God from the angel's hand. Then the angel took the censer, filled it with fire from the altar, and threw it to the earth. And there were noises, thunderings, lightnings, and an earthquake.

The gathered prayers of the Church are shown here ascending to the Lord, and bringing about a response of violent judgment from God, as the rest of Revelation chapter 8 and all of chapter 9 show us. In response to the worshipping Church's gathered prayers, God pours out upon the rebellious world hail, fire, darkness, a falling star which poisons the sea, demonic locusts, and other woes. Prayer is a weapon, since it moves God to act on behalf of His People in accordance with His Purposes. Prayer is a resource and a weapon (more on prayer further on in the book).

We're frequently uncomfortable with the idea of conflict as Christians, but let us consider what Jesus says in Matthew 10:34-39:

Do not think that I came to bring peace on earth. I did not come to bring peace but a sword. For I have come to 'set a man against his father, a daughter against her mother, and a daughter-in-law against her mother-in-law'; and 'a man's enemies will be those of his own household.' He who loves father or mother more than Me is not worthy of Me. And he who loves son or daughter more than Me is not worthy of Me. And he who does not take his cross and follow after Me is not worthy of Me. He who finds his life will lose it, and he who loses his life for My sake will find it.

The sword that Jesus brings is a conflict of loyalties that results whenever *any* relationship—family, belief-system, government, career, etc.—seeks to win ultimate commitment that belongs to Christ alone. Any relationship or entity which is dominated by the world-system of Satan must, to that extent, be viewed as at odds with the Kingdom of God, and conflict between the two will inevitably ensue.

By being joined to the Lord Jesus, we are unavoidably made citizens of Christ's Kingdom, and become soldiers in the war on the devil's world-system, and thus targets of Satan. However, even though we have become enemies of the devil, we have always been in his sights, even when we were his subjects, when he visited his evil on us as he wished. We will either, in this life, be the helpless pawns of a cruel fallen angel or his Holy Spirit-empowered enemy. Our only peace is to be found in loving service to Christ, who, as He Himself points out, "has overcome the world-system" (John 16:33). As 1 John 5:4-5 tells us of Satan's world-system: "For whatever is born of God overcomes the world. And this is the victory that has overcome the world—our faith. Who is he who overcomes the world, but he who believes that Jesus is the Son of God?" Because Jesus has defeated Satan, we share by faith in His Victory and His Authority.

We have all been born in the midst of an ancient and implacable war, but in Christ we are enabled to not only take part in the Eternal Purposes and Victory of God, but to be ourselves fulfilled in our created purpose, know life and peace in this world, and to be agents of freedom for a humanity enslaved in darkness—to be what God intended us to be.

We've seen some of the principal weapons which God has prepared for us to use as the Liberating Army of Christ: the Bible, our authority over Satan and his world-system in Jesus' Name, and prayer. These weapons make us, the Church, a Weapon, and help fit us to fight the dark powers.

Jesus said of His Mission, "The Spirit of the LORD is upon Me, because He has anointed Me to preach the Gospel to the poor; He has sent Me to heal the brokenhearted, to proclaim liberty to the captives and recovery of sight to the blind, to set at liberty those who are oppressed." This is also our task, since we are to do the same works that Jesus did (John 14:12), and it is for this task that God has made the Church the Pillar and Ground of the Truth. We are those who are to teach and live out the Word of God, the Blueprint and Marching Orders for life, and Christ has given us the authority and tools to be the Weapon to defeat the evil one, and be the Liberating Force for the sin-enslaved world.

CHAPTER 6

WHERE DO WE
WORSHIP?

Jesus told us, "To whom much is given, from him much is required" (Luke 12:48), and I'm trying to give you, Christian, as much as I can, so that you're on the hot-seat. Too late now. You've already learned a lot in the preceding chapters. You're already in deeper than you may have wanted to be: you've been tar-babied in.

My purpose is to redeem the time, not to waste it. I don't want this book to be just another lame waste-of-time where the reader fulfills some vague religious duty-impulse, and teaches us just enough truth that fulfills a religious yearning, but doesn't make him or her uncomfortable enough to change in the Light of God's Word.

My hope is that your life will *change*, so that you aren't just another unengaged Christian who is only concerned with getting through life with as little difficulty as possible, but who lives guilty and confused about who he or she is in relation to God and the world, and who never fulfill their destiny as members of the Church, and never experience freedom as they should.

I want to see believers changed into people whose lives are *filled* with the explosive, revolutionary, world-liberating Power of God, so that the Glory of God will dwell on their lives, and the lives of your friends and families, and those to whom they minister, so that they, so that *you*, will be all the things we've talked about, one of those whom God romances, the Body and Family and Temple and Home of God, the Weapon and conquering Army of God. These aren't just *ideas*; these are *ways to live*, altogether a *way of life*. I'm talking about God's Word *changing* your life and the world *forever*, for the rest of your life and *beyond*.

You're going to live *forever*. Get used to the idea. Even those in our midst who are *not* believers in Christ will live forever. Everyone will live forever, either in the Light of unbelievable Glory or in unremitting, unending, fearful pain and darkness; but we will *all* live forever, one way or the other. What we do now with our lives will determine what happens, even for Christians, since the way we live affects rewards and so forth after death.

What you do with your life now will have impact on your eternity. This is truth. Jesus says, "The Words that I speak to you, they are Spirit, and they are Life" (John 6:63). His Words are more important than anything else. They're more important than anything else you'll ever learn.

The things I'm writing about are only important to the extent that what I teach matches what Jesus says. So, *learn* His Word. Hide it in your heart. Commit it to memory. *Ingest* it. Meditate on it. Learn these things, please; don't forget them. Put them into practice. I wish I had been taught these things *years* before I learned them. Take advantage of these things.

Just because you're not a pastor, or a deacon, etc., you shouldn't think of yourself as a peripheral or unimportant part of Christ's Body. You *are* the Church; you are the Liberation Front. You are the future. So learn and practice these things. I *promise* you if you'll learn these things and put them into practice, it will not only radically transform your life and the lives of the people you know, but you will also help transform the world. I promise. Otherwise, I wouldn't waste our collective time writing this book.

First Corinthians 3:23 tells us: "And you are Christ's, and Christ is God's." And Colossians 3:3 says: "For you died, and your life is hidden with Christ in God." We share by faith both the Death and Life of the Lord Jesus, as Scripture tells us in Romans 6:3-9 and Galatians 2:20. Our life is hidden in Christ even now.

Where is Jesus now? Ephesians 1:19-23 tells us:

> [W]hat is the exceeding greatness of His power toward us
> who believe, according to the working of His mighty power
> which He worked in Christ when He raised Him from the
> dead and seated Him at His right hand in the heavenly
> places, far above all principality and power and might and
> dominion, and every name that is named not only in this
> age but also in that which is to come. And He put all things
> under His feet, and gave Him to be head over all things to
> the church, which is His body, the fullness of Him who fills
> all in all.

The Lord Jesus is now seated at the Right Hand of the Father, ruling over all things from His Heavenly Throne. Further, Ephesians 2:4-7 says:

> But God, who is rich in mercy, because of His great love with
> which He loved us, even when we were dead in trespasses,
> made us alive together with Christ (by grace you have been
> saved), and raised us up together, and made us sit together
> in the heavenly places in Christ Jesus, that in the ages to
> come He might show the exceeding riches of His grace in
> His kindness toward us in Christ Jesus.

This means that you, as a Christian, are now seated *with* Christ and *in* Christ at the Right Hand of the Father in Heaven.

This is a very mystical thing. Let me ask you something: How true is the Bible? How real are the things the Bible teaches? How trustworthy are the Scriptures? I ask these questions because I know many who read these words are saying to themselves, "Uh...you know...I don't *feel* like I'm sitting at the Right Hand of the Father..." Your senses are telling you you're not. Your mind is telling you you're not. The Lord knows our society is telling you you're not. So who are you going to believe?

This is the thing: The Bible is truer than what you *think* and what you *feel* and what you think you know. "My Words are Spirit and Life," says Jesus (John 6:63). The Bible is about *reality*, the reality of what God, the world, and your relationship to these things and everything else that exists actually is. When it tells you something like, "You are seated in Christ at the Right Hand of the Father," if you were a gambler, you could put money on it. (you might, of course, find it difficult to collect on your bet until after the Resurrection, especially if the person you bet with was not a Christian).

We need to fix this truth in our minds. Hebrews chapter 11 gives us a long list of people like Noah, Abraham, Moses, and others, all of whom were people who lived in earnest expectation of seeing all the great mysteries that would be unfolded in the future according to God's Word. However, they never in their lifetimes on earth saw these things (as Hebrews 11:13 informs us), yet *still* they spent their lives in belief in God's Promises that those things *would* come, risking their reputations, riches, and even *lives* in commitment to the truth of those Divine Promises.

Hebrews 11:39-40 further says that *we* are the ones on whom the mysteries the ancients longed for, lived for, and *died* for have come, the mysteries of Christ in us, the Hope of Glory (Colossians 1:27), of our access to God Himself through Jesus' Ascended Humanity (Hebrews 10:19-22), all benefits won for us in Christ, all of which we *know* about, Jesus having revealed them to us in Himself and His Word. You Christians who are reading these words know things that Abraham and Moses didn't know while they were alive on the earth, things they *longed* to know, but didn't.

These things have been revealed to *you*. Don't take them lightly. The greatest men in the world *longed* to know the things that so many of us take for granted, or cavalierly think we have the right to disbelieve on the strength of our own sin-distorted perspectives, thoughts, emotions, and experiences.

Who is your God? Your sin-hazed thoughts, emotions, and experiences (in other words, *yourself*), or the Perfect God Who has spoken in His Word, and Who cannot lie (as Titus 1:2 says)? In whom do you trust and believe? Yourself, or the God Who tells us only truth? How you answer that question governs your destiny beyond this life, and your effectiveness within this life.

Understand that this *is* the fulcrum of the revolution of being the Liberation Front for the world, that you would trust the Perspective and Word of God above your own. This is the question that Father Adam and Mother Eve failed to answer correctly, spinning us all down to the Curse and death, and which Christ Jesus has raised us up in Him to answer correctly by His Power, as *He* answered it. This is the single most damaging and threatening thing to Satan's illegitimate kingdom: that we would believe God's Perspective, His Word, above our own, and act in accordance with it.

One of those mysteries revealed to us is that, since Jesus has risen from the dead, and we have been baptized by His Spirit into Him, His Life is now *our* life, and we are now seated in Him at the Right Hand of the Father, as He dwells in us by His Spirit, connecting us as His Body to that Place in Heaven where He sits and rules. This is a *radical* truth, that a human being could be the Habitation of God, and that a Human Being (Christ in His Humanity) is sitting on the Right Hand of God, and that you and I, and all Christians, are seated on the Right Hand of the Father in Christ Jesus.

First Peter 2: 4-5, 9 tells us:

Coming to Him as to a living stone, rejected indeed by men, but chosen by God and precious, you also, as living stones, are being built up a spiritual house, a holy priesthood, to offer up spiritual sacrifices acceptable to God through Jesus Christ... But you are a chosen generation, a royal priesthood, a holy nation, His own special people, that you may proclaim the praises of Him who called you out of darkness into His marvelous light.

You, Twenty-First Century American believer, this is speaking of *you*. You are a king and a priest, a member of "a Royal Priesthood," according to God's Word which cannot be broken (John 10:35). That's what God's Word says about His People, about *all* of His People. If you are a Christian, you *are* a priest. What does that mean? What does a priest do? A priest worships his God. He also does one other thing, as part of his worship: A priest represents his God to men, and he represents men to God. These are the two basic things a priest does.

That's what you're supposed to do It's what you *are*. Part of where you find your destiny and meaning as a person, O Christian, is that you are a priest. (And not just a priest, but a royal priest, which you should research). The function of a priest is further illuminated by what we see in Exodus 5:1.

Afterward Moses and Aaron went in and told Pharaoh, "Thus says The LORD God of Israel: 'Let My people go, that they may hold a feast to Me in the wilderness.'"

If you know the history of the Exodus, you know that God did a number of extraordinary and radical things to Pharaoh's Egypt, so that Pharaoh would release the nation of Israel from slavery. God sent ten plagues on Egypt, the last of which killed all the Egyptian firstborn. Why did God do this? What did He want? Exodus 5:1 tells us. He wanted Israel to go out and offer worship to Him (the feast mentioned here was a Holy Feast involving sacrifices, corporate liturgical action, and so forth). That's the reason God gave both to the pagan Pharaoh *and* to Israel.

This was so important to God that He not only wiped out the Egyptian firstborn, but also killed off the whole Egyptian army in the Red Sea when they pursued the departing Israelites (Exodus 14). You might say, in God's List of Priorities, His People's worship of Him came pretty high, and He was fairly determined they would be able to do so. This is what God's People *do*: they *worship* God. Even in the Old Testament, Israel was a nation of priests (Exodus 19:6), just as (surprise, surprise) the New Testament Church is. The entire People of God were to worship Him together. This is the main point: worship is our reason for being.

Why are we to bear the Gospel to people? Why are we to call them into the Kingdom of Light to be discipled there? What does God want? Same as it ever was—He wants them to *worship* Him. What will you be doing after the Resurrection of the Dead, when you're in your new body in the Presence of God in the New Heavens and Earth? Worshipping. God places a high premium on worship. It was important enough to Him that He was willing to kill numbers of people (all created in His Image, remember) that were restraining His People so that His Nation of Priests could be freed to worship Him.

It's also important enough to Him that He was willing to come and *die*, so His People, the Church, would be freed from their terminal slavery to sin, the world, and the devil, so they could make an Exodus into His Presence to worship Him. That's how important worship is to God.

> Therefore it was necessary that the copies of the things in the Heavens should be purified with these, but the heavenly things themselves with better sacrifices than these. For Christ has not entered the holy places made with hands, which are copies of the true, but into heaven itself, now to appear in the presence of God for us (Hebrews 9:23-24).

This passage is talking about the *Ascension*. When Jesus rose into Heaven after His Resurrected Sojourn with His Disciples (Acts 1:9-11), He went into the place in Heaven called in the Epistle to the Hebrews "the Tabernacle" and "the Heavenly Tabernacle." If you know anything about the Old Testament worship that God commanded Israel to perform, you know it was unbelievably complicated, with specific things in specific places at specific times to be done accompanied by specific actions performed by specific people. This Tabernacle worship later transferred over to the Temple in Jerusalem, as well (which actually *housed* the Tabernacle).

Very complicated. Why? Did God just want to make people jump through some hoops? No. What the Israelites were worshipping within during Old Covenant times (e.g., the Tabernacle and the Temple) was a *model* of the Real Temple which was in Heaven. What was the point? They were building a Model on the earth, at God's Explicit Direction, of what Heaven is like. That's why this passage tells us that the copies of the Heavenly Tabernacle were cleansed by the blood of animals, which pointed to the fact that when Jesus died, He would (as He has) consecrate the Heavenly Tabernacle for the real worship to begin. Jesus went into Heaven, and is seated at the Father's Right Hand, having cleansed and consecrated the Heavenly Temple with His Blood, now overseeing and presiding over the worship in Heaven. This is why Christ is called a High Priest, for He has gone into Heaven to worship God, and to represent men to God, as He has represented God to men. Jesus has gone into the True Heavenly Tabernacle to lead the worship before God's Throne.

By that will we have been sanctified through the offering of the Body of Jesus Christ once for all. And every priest stands ministering daily and offering repeatedly the same sacrifices, which can never take away sins. But this Man, after He had offered one sacrifice for sins forever, sat down at the right hand of God, from that time waiting till His enemies are made His footstool. For by one offering He has perfected forever those who are being sanctified. But the Holy Spirit also witnesses to us; for after He had said before, "This is the covenant that I will make with them after those days, says the LORD: I will put My laws into their hearts, and in their minds I will write them," then He adds, "Their sins and their lawless deeds I will remember no more." Now where there is remission of these, there is no longer an offering for sin. Therefore, brethren, having boldness to enter the Holiest by the Blood of Jesus, by a new and living way which He consecrated for us, through the veil, that is, His Flesh, and having a High Priest over the house of God, let us draw near with a true heart in full assurance of faith, having our hearts sprinkled from an evil conscience and our bodies washed with pure water (Hebrews 10:10-22).

What does this mean? It means we enter the Heavens by the Spirit's Power through the Ascended Humanity of Christ. "The Holiest" here is the aforementioned Heavenly Tabernacle, where Christ is seated, through "a new and living way...that is, His Flesh."

We go into Heaven through the Humanity of Christ (the Veil of His Flesh, Which was torn for us as the Veil of the Temple was torn open at His Death in the Old Covenant Temple, showing He had thrown open by His Torn Body the way for men to go into the Holy of Holies through *Him*; cf. Matthew 27: 50-53). Why do you think it is we're seated at the Right Hand of the Father in Him? Positionally, we're already seated in Christ in the Presence of God. And we as a People have access to God because of what Jesus has done by the Sacrifice of His Body and Blood.

His Life has become *our* life (we live out, remember, *His* Story), and we, spiritually, are seated in Him at the Right Hand of the Father. That means that we can go into *Heaven* to worship. That's pretty out there, Kemper, you say. I'm glad you brought that up. Attend to John 4:19-24:

> The woman said to him, "Sir, I perceive that you are a prophet. Our fathers worshiped on this mountain, and you Jews say that in Jerusalem is the place where one ought to worship." Jesus said to her, "Woman, believe Me, the hour is coming when you will neither on this mountain, nor in Jerusalem, worship the Father. You worship what you do not know; we know what we worship, for salvation is of the Jews. But the hour is coming, and now is, when the true worshippers will worship the Father in spirit and truth; for the Father is seeking such to worship Him. God is Spirit, and those who worship Him must worship in spirit and truth."

This passage is normally taught as though if you worship in *spirit*, you really *feel* something (sort of like "school spirit" in high school). That is *not* what worshipping in spirit means, and it doesn't answer the question the woman asked, which was, "*Where* do we worship?" Jesus is answering her question when He says, "Those who worship Him must worship in Spirit and in Truth." He wasn't talking about a way you *feel* or what you *believe*. He was talking about a *place*. What could *that* mean? So glad you thought to ask that question.

Hebrews 12:22-24 (my translation) answers that question:

> But you have come to Mount Zion and to the city of the living God, the heavenly Jerusalem, and to innumerable angels in festal gathering, to the general assembly and church of the firstborn who are registered in heaven, to God the Judge of all, to the spirits of just men made perfect, to Jesus the Mediator of the new covenant, and to the blood of sprinkling that speaks better things than that of Abel.

You should be aware that here (as in most places in the New Testament) the "you" is actually the second person plural, "y'all," as we say in Texas (and most American regions have some version of this: "you'uns" or "youse guys" or some such word). So, "Y'all've come to Mount Zion, the Heavenly Jerusalem," e.g., the place where Jesus is seated, the Heavens where the True Tabernacle contains

Christ on His Throne at the Father's Right Hand is how this should be understood, as the "you" here is a plurality.

"...to innumerable angels in festal gathering," in other words, thousands and thousands of angels dressed to party (as the Greek of the text intimates here). "...to the General Assembly and Church of the Firstborn who are registered in Heaven," e.g., those whose names are written in the Books of Life (Revelation 20:12), the Church. The implications of this verse (verse 23) is that it means not just the people who are alive now, but the *entire* Church across time as well as space. This means *all* the people who have ever been or ever will be part of the Church. How can this be? Let's look on in the verse.

"...to God the Judge of all" is pretty straight ahead, meaning-wise: God is there. "...to the spirits of just men made perfect." What does that mean? It means they're *dead*. Dead people ("I see dead people"). For instance, those believers spoken of earlier in Hebrews chapter 11: Noah, Abraham, Moses, etc. Finally, "...to Jesus the Mediator of the New Covenant, and to the Blood of sprinkling...," the Ascended Lord Jesus and His Atoning Blood.

This is a description of the Throne Room, into which Jesus has ascended and where He presides over the worship in Heaven. This epistle, Hebrews, was written to be read to a group of Christians gathered for worship on the Lord's Day (there were no printing presses then, of course). This passage is contrasted in this chapter with the Old Covenant worship (Hebrews 12: 18-21) to tell believers that when they go to worship, they don't just worship on the earth (as believers did in Old Covenant times). Neither do we even just worship in this time.

The Holy Spirit draws us in worship through the Rent Veil of Christ's Flesh into the Heavenly Tabernacle which transcends time and space. When we worship, we are drawn into the Domain of the Spirit, the Throne Room of God Himself.

You may know that the Early Church had worship that was somewhat different from that of most modern Evangelical churches. This ancient form of worship was (and still is) called *liturgical* worship, and it was set up according to the patterns of worship seen in the glimpses of Heavenly Worship given us in Scripture (such as Isaiah 6, Ezekiel 1 and 10, and Revelation 4-5). The mainspring of the Early Christian understanding of worship was driven by the realization that, when they gathered to worship, the Holy Spirit caused Heaven and earth to merge.

Jesus says, "Where two or three are gathered together in My Name, there am I in the midst of them" (Matthew 18:20), and this is not just a metaphor. In worship, Heaven and earth *fuse*, and we come together into the Courts of Heaven through Christ, where we are already seated in Jesus at the Father's Right Hand. We do our worshipping in Heaven. When we gather for formal worship, something very mystical happens: the Holy Spirit draws us into the

Sphere of the Heavens. Your senses will frequently tell you that this is not true. Again, what will we believe?

The reason the Church in centuries past fixed their buildings so ornately, and the reason they followed the patterns of worship they did, was that they wanted to conform their worship patterns to those of the Scriptural accounts of those in the Heavenly worship (since, they reasoned, we worship there), and they wanted to point out architecturally that they worshipped in the Heavenly Places, the most beautiful Place in the Cosmos.

The whole Church, at every point in time, is joined through the Christ Who is the Head of His Body (across time and space) to the Heavenly Throne Room. God, Who is bigger than all time, and Whose Throne sits at the center of Reality like a greased ball-bearing around which Reality wheels, is present in His Throne Room to all times simultaneously, every time at all times, and the entire Church comes together beyond time at the same time, right there in God's Presence! This is a heavy, radical truth.

The next time you're sitting in worship, bored out of your gourd, it would be well to remember where you *truly* are, because you're not just sitting in a building somewhere; you're sitting in the Presence of the Living God and His Christ, with angels and *all* of the saints. Your senses and your rationalistic mind, which have been trained to deny the supernatural, is going to try to reject the truth. We, however, must see with the Eyes of the Spirit the vision He has infallibly revealed in Scripture. Scripture is realer than what you think, you know. Can't buy it?

"Blessed are those who have not seen, and yet have believed," said Jesus to doubting Thomas (John 20:29). He was talking about His Resurrection from the Dead. Did you see it? No. But you still believe? You believe that part of Scripture. Why do you not believe the parts we've been looking at? Consistency is a good thing. If you can accept the Mysteries of the Virgin Birth, the Resurrection, the Trinity, and the Incarnation, why is it difficult to accept your position in Christ by Whom you worship in Heaven?

"I was in the Spirit on the Lord's Day" (Revelation 1:10). Did John the Revelator suddenly feel good? That is not what John is saying. He went to a *place*. John went on to write (about the same Lord's Day, or Sunday, we would say now) in Revelation 4:1-2:

> After these things I looked, and behold, a door standing open in heaven. And the first voice which I heard was like a trumpet speaking with me, saying, "Come up here, and I will show you things which must take place after this." Immediately I was in the Spirit; and behold, a throne set in heaven, and One sat on the throne.

Remember the answer to the question that the woman at the well in John 4 asked Jesus about *where* we were to worship, and He said those who worship Him must worship

Him in Spirit and in Truth? Here John writes of the same place, since he was in the Spirit on a Sunday, and what did he see? He saw the worship in Heaven. The Heavenly Courts are where the Spirit and the Truth are, and where those who would worship God correctly do worship Him.

Revelation, chapters 4 and 5, which is what John recorded seeing on that long-ago Sunday, show us what Heavenly Worship is like. The hymns and anthems and confessions and actions of these passages (and those of Isaiah 6 and Ezekiel chapters 1 and 10, which describe the same Heavenly Tabernacle) were taken up and repeated and enacted by the Early Church in their worship orders, their liturgies, because, they reasoned, if we worship in Heaven, we should conform our worship to Heaven's, since Heaven's Worship is the prototype for all corporate worship.

Today, in the United States, we all want to go to worship to *get* something *from* it. We want to go primarily to get a blessing, or to enjoy the music, or to be taught, or whatever. But worship, you see, is not *primarily* for *us*, priest of the Church. Worship is primarily for God, for *His* Pleasure; it is intended to be a Command Performance to please *Him*. We are backwards, in our time, in our understanding of these things. All we're worried about in worship is what we're going to get out of it; we're generally not worried in the least what *God* wants from it. We do things that amuse *us* in worship. What do you think the denizens of Heaven (the angels and saints) or God Himself think of the fact that we refuse to orient our worship to Him? Don't you imagine them saying, "They just don't get it?"

Most of our bad ideas about worship stem from the fact that we no longer believe we worship in Heaven, and lacking the perspective of Scripture which reveals what's *really* going on, we focus on ourselves. We think it's all about us personally, not about all of us together, and not about what pleases God. Don't get me wrong. Enjoying the music, being blessed, and learning are all good things in themselves, but they are secondary, flowing from, and conditioned and informed by, the primary focus on pleasing God.

We're called, as priests, to go through our Great High Priest, Christ, into the Tabernacle in Heaven Sunday by Sunday to offer our worship in the Presence of God in accordance with the patterns of the worship in Heaven to thereby enact a Command Performance to please the God Who values worship so much that He freed a nation of millions to worship Him, killing people along the way to aid that goal, and Who came Himself to die so that people could offer Him worship.

It's a big deal to God, and it ought to be a big deal to us, the royal priesthood of Christ.

CHAPTER SEVEN

WHAT HAPPENS IN WORSHIP?

In the last chapter, we saw the mysterious truth that we worship in the Very Presence of the Triune God, as the Spirit lifts us as a people through Christ (the same Spirit Who applied the Saving Effect of Christ's Atoning Sacrifice to us) so we can worship before the Father's Face. We also saw that our worship should *primarily* be for God's Pleasure and Enjoyment. We saw as well that there were secondary effects of worship that come as a by-product of primary worship which do benefit the worshipper(s). It is these secondary effects that sometimes become the idolatrous goal of self-fixated pseudo-worship.

However, the truth that correctly oriented worship *does* bring beneficial effects is the foundation for the temptation to twist such effects into being the goal of self-fixated worship. These benefits and blessings, when legitimately obtained, serve to shape and inform every one of the modes of the Church we've explored so far. In this chapter we'll consider some of the specific ways that worship affects the various modes of existence of the Church.

The author of the Epistle to the Hebrews wrote to his beleaguered flock to be "not forsaking the assembling together of ourselves together, as is the habit of some" (Hebrews 10:25), a verse concerning the corporate Lord's Day worship of the Church, and which has been utilized for ages as a clarion call for faithful worship attendance. Of course, this verse is not just intended to be a heavy-handed guilt trip to manipulate an individual's brute attendance on Sundays, but should be viewed in the larger context of the teaching on worship laid out in Hebrews and culminating in verses 22-24 of chapter 12, in the setting of the Spirit-energized ascent to the Courts of Heaven through Jesus, with the attendant emphasis on worship that is a ministry of praise and adoration to the Trinity, and the consequent outpouring of Blessings on the worshipping Church. To forsake corporate worship is not only to fail to give God the worship He is due, but also to miss out on the gifts and benefits God gives in response to worship: to equip the Church to serve Him and advance His Purposes in the world.

It likely goes without saying (but I'll say it anyway) that worship in the Very Presence of God is obviously tied in to the Church's existence as a Temple. We've seen that the Church is, individually and corporately, inhabited by the Holy Spirit, Who is building us (individually and corporately) into His Temple (Ephesians 2:19-22). We've further seen that the Church is lifted into the Shekinah, the Heavenly Tabernacle which is the Domain of the Spirit (John 4:21-24; Hebrews 10:19-20; 12:22-24), the heart of Reality, the source of the Kingdom which will transform the Cosmos into the Temple of the New Heavens and the New Earth (Matthew 19:28; 1 Corinthians 7:31; 1 John 2:8, 17; Revelation 21-22).

In that place, the assembled Church fulfills its responsibilities as a nation of kings and priests (1 Peter 2:5, 9; Revelation 1:6; 5:10), since priests bear the responsibility to represent men to God and God to men. The first is fulfilled in worship and adoration toward God, as the praises of men are delivered by the Church to the Lord in His Presence (as we see in the visions of the Heavenly Service in Revelation 4:10-11; 5:9-14; 7:10-12; 15:3-4). The Church is to "in everything give thanks, for this is the Will of God in Christ Jesus for you" (1 Thessalonians 5:18).

However, this is also shown in the concern delivered in prayer to God for men, which is seen in Revelation 5:8 (where the prayers of the saints are the incense which fills the golden bowls, the censers, in God's Presence) and 6:10

(which we've seen is a prayer for God to act in Judgment against the enemies of God and His People). These acts of corporate and individual worship are enjoined throughout the New Testament, as in Romans 12:12 (where the Church is commanded to be "continuing steadfastly in prayer"), Ephesians 6:18 (which commands that we be "praying always with all prayer and supplication in the Spirit, being watchful to this end with all perseverance and supplication for all the saints"), Philippians 4:6 ("Be anxious for nothing, but in everything by prayer and supplication, with thanksgiving, let your requests be made known to God; and the peace of God, which surpasses all understanding, will guard your hearts and minds through Christ Jesus"), 1 Thessalonians 5:17 (which commands us simply to "pray without ceasing"), 1 Timothy 2:1-3 ("Therefore I exhort first of all that supplications, prayers, intercessions, and giving of thanks be made for all men, for kings and all who are in authority, that we may lead a quiet and peaceable life in all godliness and reverence. For this is good and acceptable in the sight of God our Savior"), 1 Timothy 4:5 ("For every creature of God is good, and nothing is to be refused if it is received with thanksgiving; for it is sanctified by the word of God and prayer," this passage itself a sort of mandate for the Church), 1 Peter 4:7 (where we are commanded to "be serious and watchful in your prayers"), and James 5:16 (we are to "pray for one another, that you may be healed. The effective, fervent prayer of a righteous man avails much"). There are, of course, others, and I haven't even touched on the Old Testament passages concerning our responsibility and privilege to pray.

We are to pray ceaselessly, interceding for each other, ourselves, and those around us, fulfilling our calling as a nation of priests, those who pray and those who worship, becoming individually and all together the Temple we are called to be. Our worship, flowing from our individual into our corporate worship, is to further flow out into the world, praying for those who inhabit it that they too might be drawn into the Church, offer praise to their Maker and Redeemer, and take part in the outward flow of God's Grace which will transform the Fallen Cosmos into a New Heavens and Earth, a river of the Knowledge of the Lord which will one day cover the earth as the waters cover the sea (Isaiah 11:9; Habakkuk 2:14).

Not only are the Temple priests to represent men to God in praise and prayer, but they are also to represent God to men, a task engaged by the preaching and enacting of God's Word, which takes place in its foundational sense in the Presence of the Lord Who caused it to be written in the first place (2 Timothy 3:16-17; 2 Peter 1:19-21), as Scripture is rehearsed and taught in the context of the Patterns of Heavenly Worship which are shaped by, and which interpret, the Word of God for the worshippers. Worship is where our ideas about God, men, and the world are learned and honed, and the preaching of Scripture is an integral and primary element of that formation, and of its subsequent development in our understanding. This shouldn't surprise us, since the Spirit Who inspired and inhabits the Scriptures is also the One Who inhabits us as His Temple and connects us to Christ our Head as His Body.

In the Heavenly Liturgy revealed in the Book of Revelation (Revelation contains more quotations of different parts of Scripture than any other book in the New Testament), we see in chapter 15:3 the worshippers quoting (in a song, no less, much as the original was) the Song of Moses from Exodus 15, and in chapter 4:3 the Trisagion ("Holy, Holy, Holy, Lord God Almighty...") from Isaiah 6 is utilized. In Revelation 5:1-8, we see Christ the Lamb of God proclaiming and interpreting the Scroll of God's Word, which sets in motion actions for the rest of chapter 5 and throughout chapter 6. Not only does Scripture permeate the Heavenly Worship, but the interpretation and understanding of it provokes change in the worshippers and the world itself, as it always does. This is one of the reasons we proclaim and sing the Word of God in our worship.

The Patterns of the Heavenly Worship, replicated in our worship on the earth, themselves tell the Gospel and help us to see the pattern of our lives in the Patterns of the Life of Jesus, to Whose Life we are joined by His

Spirit (Romans 6:1-13; Galatians 2:20; 5:24-25; etc.). The Sacraments, which also attest what Christ has done for us, and carry His Grace, also are conducted in the worship of the Church. It's also true that the exercise of the spiritual gifts takes place as the Body of Christ gathers in the Presence of her Head. You'll note that all these activities involve our bodies, our physicality, and matter itself, just as the Lord Jesus was Incarnate as One Person both Physical and Spiritual (as we are), teaching us that the Scriptures address *all* of life, the entire spectrum of life in the Cosmos (and beyond).

These actions and events, energized by the Holy Spirit, are the context in which we hear and understand the Word of God, and see how it applies to God, men, and the world, and prepares us to be the Ground and Pillar of the Truth, the Church which preaches and enacts what the Scriptures teach to all who will see and hear. Worship makes it possible for us to *be* the Pillar and Ground of Truth we have been created to become.

It is the Holy Spirit Who also energizes the aforementioned Gifts which He has distributed to each member of the Body as He sees fit (Romans 12:4-8; 1 Corinthians 12:1-31; 14:1-22), and, though those Gifts are to benefit the Body at all times, this is especially true when the Church is gathered in the Presence of Christ the Lord to bring about the edification (a word which means "building up") of the members of His Body to accomplish the purposes to which He has called her (1 Corinthians 14:26-40). The Gifts aid both physical and spiritual needs, keeping the Church in health and preparation in both spheres, finding their fullest expression during worship when the Body is gathered together.

The exercise of the Gifts toward one another to help one another to health and well-being spiritually and otherwise strengthens the entire Body, building the Body up in our relationship both toward our head, Christ Jesus, as well as toward the other members, thus, having both vertical and horizontal emphases, emphases which foster unity with both God and man. That unity, since it builds up the Body, extends across time and space, since the Church is both processional (proceeding from the Work of the Holy Spirit, as He calls people to believe) and successional (successive generations springing from previous ones), and the Church's health benefits those who come next after each generation of believers.

The love manifested in the exercise of worship helps to cement the relationships of the Church as the Family of God, all gathered together around the Father through the Ascended Humanity of Jesus their Brother and Joint-Heir, a reunion, as we've seen, with the entire Church across all time and space, which takes place every Lord's Day when the congregations gather in worship.

The love of family is to manifest itself in forgiveness toward one another, since Jesus said, "For if you forgive others their trespasses, your heavenly Father will also forgive you, but if you do not forgive men their trespasses, neither will your Father forgive your trespasses" (Matthew 6:14-15)—scary words that show just how seriously the Lord takes relationships, and how important to Him is the maintenance of those relationships. Two passages tie the importance of forgiveness and reconciliation (and there are others, as well) to worship. Mark 11:25 tells us: "And whenever you stand praying, if you have anything against anyone, forgive him, that your Father in heaven may also forgive you your trespasses. But if you do not forgive, neither will your Father in heaven forgive your trespasses." The other passage tying reconciliation to worship is Matthew 5:23-24: "Therefore if you bring your gift to the altar, and there remember that your brother has something against you, leave your gift there before the altar, and go your way. First be reconciled to your brother, and then come and offer your gift."

Here we see a couple of things. First, when approaching God in worship (in this case, standing to pray to Him, as was the ancient custom, and bringing an offering to the altar), our relationships with one another can interrupt our relationship with Him. Second, just as a relationship can be broken between Christians, yet there can be reconciliation between them by repentance and forgiveness, so the relationship of man and God can be repaired by such a process, and maintained by an attitude of, and the willingness to live in a state of, forgiveness.

Why do our relationships with other humans so affect our relationship with God? We are made in the Image of God (Genesis 1:26-27), intended to mirror, on a creaturely level, the Triune God Whose Image we bear. The Lord exists in an Eternal Relationship of Love and Peace between His Three Persons (Father, Son, and Holy Spirit), and we are meant to show that same Love and Peace between the members of the Family of God, so disruption in the relationships between believers shows a picture of God which is untrue, of disruption between God's Persons (which is untrue because impossible, in light of the Perfections possessed and shared between the Triune Persons). For this sin (for such is what unforgiveness truly is), God takes massive umbrage.

Yet you might say, "Well, the Persons of the Trinity are Perfect and Unfallen, while we humans are both sinful and Fallen, so how can we be expected to image God perfectly?" The answer to this question is directly related to the other major way we also image the Lord in our mutual relationships. While it is true that we once were spiritually powerless to overcome sin (Ephesians 2:1-3), we have been set free from the iron dominion of sin in our lives by having been regenerated in Christ (Ephesians 2:4-10; Galatians 2:20). This was made possible by the Redemption accomplished by the Sacrifice of the Incarnate

Lord Jesus on the Cross, winning forgiveness from God for us by taking God's Righteous Wrath on Himself, so that we *could* be forgiven.

That Divine Forgiveness is foundational to the Family Relationship we have with God the Father and one another (since such a relationship with God and one another would be impossible without the forgiveness offered in and through Jesus), and our relationships with one another in the Family and Body are to bear witness that they are the product of (as well as that they produce) forgiveness. If our relationships are not characterized by forgiveness and reconciliation, then they seem to deny the reality of the very Forgiveness that makes them possible. People can't always see our relationship with the Lord, but it's not difficult to see divisions among the members of the Family on earth.

However, even beyond the bad witness such divisions give to unbelievers, to carry such divisions and sinful attitudes into the Presence of God in worship, where we offer our thanks for God's Forgiveness while professing to offer all we are to Him and praying for His Favor, is an insult and a rank denial of the fact that Christ *has* won forgiveness for us and made us the Family of our God and Father, since we are to live in forgiveness toward others, even as Jesus showed toward the very men who crucified Him (Luke 23:33-34). We are to live as a Family forged by the Forgiveness of God in Christ, extending the same forgiveness toward one another that God shows us in Christ. If we refuse to do so, it is only because we prefer to love ourselves, and to do what we want, rather than to love the Lord more than ourselves, remembering that, just as He forgave all our rebellion and darkness (for which He suffered and died), there is to be nothing done to us that we are unwilling to forgive for the Sake of Christ. And we certainly are not to give sinful offense to anyone, especially our fellow Family members. It's in worship, where we learn more deeply about Jesus and His Loving Sacrifice for us as we hear His Word and are fed from His Table in His Presence with all the gathered Family of God, that we learn the value of our relationships with our sisters and brothers, and are conditioned to live in the forgiveness of God's Family.

Now, since we've just been examining the seriousness with which God views sinful behavior by the Church, we should remind ourselves of just what is motivating His hostility toward our sin. One of His Main Motivations is Love. Just like that, we're back to Romance.

The Church is the Bride of Christ (Revelation 21:2 & 9), and, just as a human bridegroom is to be concerned primarily for the sanctification of his bride, so the Lord is dedicated to the task of making the Church, His Bride, holy, as Ephesians 5:25-27 tells us:

Husbands, love your wives, as Christ loved the church and gave himself up for her, that He might sanctify and cleanse her with the washing of water by the Word, that He might present her to Himself a glorious church, not having spot or wrinkle or any such thing, but that she should be holy and without blemish.

Of course, God is always concerned that His Bride be holy as He is Holy (Leviticus 11:44-45; 19:2 1 Peter 1:15), but why would that be? Apart from the reason that God created humanity to be reflectors to reveal Who He is, He intends for His Bride to be glorious and without blemish—He is determined that the Church be cleansed and perfect. However, the interesting thing about all this is that, since we were created to be holy reflectors of God (His Image-bearers), the holier we actually are, the freer and more fulfilled we will be. Holiness is our ultimate destiny (1 John 3:2; 1 Corinthians 15:42-49), and Christ Jesus so singularly is determined that we should be holy (and thus free and fulfilled) because He loves His Bride so much, and He wants her to be free and fulfilled. He is savagely and ruthlessly concerned to make us holy, free, and fulfilled in our relationship with Him, because He *loves* us.

Worship shows us just how much He loves His Bride, as He meets with us to give us His Promises of Love, energize the Gifts He has given to make us spiritually and physically healthier, and to feed all of His Bride (across time and space) at His Table, a Meal that anticipates the Great Wedding Feast of the Lamb (Revelation 19:6-9), the joining of all the members of the Bride with Her Bridegroom on Doomsday (and, of course, as we've seen, we worship in God's Throne-room beyond time and space, so that *every* Lord's Supper is to be a Wedding-Feast of the Lamb for His Bride). The driving force behind the Lord's Jealousy for the holiness of His Bride is Romance, and it shows in worship.

We should never lose sight of the fact that Jesus' Love for His Bride is a driving force behind His Determination to cleanse and equip us to obey Him in love (John 14:15), since this is also a path to our best well-being and freedom. To that end, the Lord forms us not only to be intercessors and prophets *for* His People and Kingdom, but also *against* His enemies and the world-system of Satan.

We saw earlier in this book (in chapter 5) that we are empowered in Christ to take authority over all Satan's power (Luke 10:19-20), and that we as Weapons wield both the proclamation of the Word, the Sword of the Spirit (Ephesians 6:17; Hebrews 4:12), and prayer (John 14:13; 15:16; 16:23) in faith (Matthew 21:21; Mark 11:23), making us, by the Power of the Spirit of Jesus, a tremendous threat to the Devil's world-system. Again, worship fits us to be a sharp and effective Weapon in the Lord's Hand, honing the tools God has given us to accomplish our assaults on the dark kingdom, and helping to fulfill our mode of being precisely as those Weapons.

As to the proclamation of the Word, which By His Power draws the captives of the Devil to allegiance to Christ, and which uncovers Satan's destructive stratagems, throwing light to dispel his darkness and, in Jesus' Name, compelling the obedience of Satan and his minions, the prophetic proclamation and teaching of Scripture as the Church gathers in the Presence of God (which is where we learn most deeply the power and meaning of the Bible, as the Holy Spirit drives this home to us in the atmosphere of affirmation, testimony, and adoration toward the Author of the Word) reinforces and deepens our grasp of the Word which is our sword against the Evil One. (This is why the failure of pastors to preach the full spectrum of the Bible's meaning and power is so destructive to the equipping of believers, and thus to the advance of Christ's Kingdom).

We've also seen in chapter 5 that prayer is to be engaged in, both in its faithful request for God to attest the truth of His Word and the power of His Kingdom by boldness in proclaiming the Scriptures accompanied by miraculous displays (Acts 4:23-31), and in terms of prayers of assault (sometimes called maledictory or imprecatory prayers) which call on God to act directly against Satan's forces (as we saw in Revelation 8:2-5). Both of the examples we looked at, in Acts 4 and Revelation 8, occurred in the context of corporate worship, of the Church gathered in

Christ's Presence, as they together interceded to ask God to act in restraining Judgment against His enemies, which, in both cases, He did.

Such prayers (and there are many such, especially in the Book of Psalms, such as Psalm 35, 68, 59, and so forth) can (and should) of course be prayed and utilized individually, but though this is true, there is a reason the Church has historically prayed these prayers in worship together, a reason laid out by Jesus in Matthew 18:18-20:

> "Assuredly, I say to you, whatever you bind on earth will be bound in heaven, and whatever you loose on earth will be loosed in heaven. Again I say to you that if two of you agree on earth concerning anything that they ask, it will be done for them by My Father in heaven. For where two or three are gathered together in My name, I am there in the midst of them."

Now, it's sometimes argued that this passage is only referring to the administration of Church Discipline, and that is the context in which Jesus utters these statements as recorded in Matthew's Gospel. However, it seems to me that the principles set out here are primarily advanced as principles referring to the *setting* of the administration of Church Discipline, and they refer, as well, to the conducting of any and all of the Church's actions and callings in worship. That being said, even if this passage *does* only refer to the administration of Church Discipline (which, in my estimation, it does not), it would still apply to the acts of warfare prayer engaged by the gathered Church. You'll note that Jesus explains the efficacy of the agreed-upon binding and loosing prayer being accomplished by the Father as being due to His Presence among the gathered worshippers. The Church historically has always seen the context of prayer (warfare/imprecatory or not) as being most effective in the primary setting of gathered worship, since Christ, who is always present with us (Matthew 28:20; Hebrews 13:5; John 10:28-29), is present with His People in ways He normally is not when they gather to do corporate worship in His Heavenly Presence. Thus, worship together offers us, as Weapons, the optimal setting to wage war in prayer.

One more observation on the efficacy of worship as a premier setting to hone the Church as Jesus' Weapon: The emphasis in worship not only on forgiveness and reconciliation (which we looked at earlier in this chapter), but also on repentance generally, is a necessary preparation to engaging the dark kingdom in war. We've seen before that we, as members of Christ's Body and His Weapon, possess derivative authority from Him over the world-system of the Devil (Luke 10:19-20). While this is absolutely the truth, we should be aware that unconfessed sin or ongoing sinful attitudes may hamper our effectiveness in utilizing our authority. Demons (and non-believing humans) are not stupid, and demons are preternaturally aware of our spiritual states without us revealing them (as Acts 19:13-17; Mark 1:23-27), (and humans are frequently more intuitive than we think). They can (and will) take issue with our exercise of authority if they know we are spiritually compromised, arguing that we are not fit to exercise such authority, or even mounting ferocious attacks in those areas of our weakness. The humans will simply (and, unfortunately, correctly in some cases) write us off as hypocrites, which definitely dulls the edge of the Weapon, as it were.

We've already looked at the spiritual havoc unforgiveness can wreak in our relationships with God and men, and any sin can actually have tremendously enervative effects on these same relationships, as well as on the exercise of our spiritual authority, which, after all, depends on the ongoing Empowerment of the Holy Spirit, Who is grieved by sin in our lives (Ephesians 4:30). This embarrassing (and potentially dangerous) situation can, of course, be avoided by ongoing repentance and confession under the Blood of Jesus (as 1 John 1:9 tells us). Worship offers a marvelous opportunity for us to examine ourselves in light of the teaching and reading of the Scriptures, our focus on Who God Is and What He has done for us, and the danger of partaking in the Lord's Supper/Eucharist/Communion without examining yourself, since uncritical taking of the Supper could result in sickness or even death, as Paul tells us in 1 Corinthians 11:27-31.

I realize that not every church celebrates the Supper weekly, or even bi-weekly or monthly, but, when they do, most churches provide a place in the service before imbibing the elements for individual and corporate repentance, yet even those who only infrequently celebrate the Supper have a time in their service for confession, even if only as part of the Invitation to non-believers to profess faith in Christ. Just as Jesus urged in Matthew 6 and Mark 11, before engaging in acts of corporate worship (standing to pray, or offering a gift at the altar [analogous to the Eucharist in New Covenant worship]), we should discipline ourselves to self-examination and repentance (and it certainly wouldn't hurt to be urged to do so corporately by our ministers in this setting) engaging in such a practice would help make sure that we possess a good conscience before God when using our authority over the Evil One. Worship is a good place to develop such a practice.

Worship, indeed, strengthens all of the modes of being of the Church we've looked at so far in this chapter (Temple, Pillar and Ground of the Truth, Body, Family, Romance, and Weapon), and this strengthening all feeds into the final mode of the Church we're looking at in this book, that of the Church as a Liberating Army. To truly be a Liberating Army, we must ourselves be free, and as we progress into being more consistently what we have been created to be in Christ, we will necessarily display more freedom in what we are and do. These modes all condition us to be a liberating Army:

The Temple mode drives us to the Presence of God to represent humanity before Him (praying and interceding for them) and to represent God to humanity, especially in the nexus of worship and adoration of the One Who has in fact freed us.

Our existence as a Family holds out to those alone and alienated a real community, a place of fellowship and love not just on the human level, but on the Divine level as well, individually and corporately in reconciled worship of the Redeeming God Who made that a possibility, desires which drive much of what mankind (even unbelieving mankind) longs for and seeks to enact.

Corollary to this is existence as Family is that of Christ's Body, which not only allows us to access supernatural Gifts of the Spirit which augment our spiritual and physical well-being, but also allows us to enter the Heavenly Worship in reconciled relationship to the Head of the Body, Jesus Christ, and to find a place of purpose and important necessity to God's Purposes in our own gifts.

The Romance with the Lord into which the Church has been drawn by His Spirit causes us to know we are deeply and eternally loved, as we go together in worship to feast with our Bridegroom, Who gives us His Promises, Gifts, and His Loving Presence, all of which teach us to love and value what He loves even more, which ultimately provides motivation to fulfill these modes in our personal and corporate existence as the Church.

To accomplish these Goals and Purposes which God has for us, we in worship learn about, and are enabled to utilize more effectively, the tools which Jesus has given us (the Word, His Authority, and prayer) so we can be the Weapon He envisions in our assault on the works of the Devil (1 John 3:8; John 14:12) and to aid the advance of His Kingdom.

Being the Pillar and Ground of the Truth, the arena wherein the Word, imbued with the Presence of the Spirit, and preached and enacted in worship before God, addresses all of life, and reveals Christ Jesus as the One "in Whom are hidden all the treasures of Wisdom and Knowledge" (Colossians 2:3), showing us Who He is, and who we are, and how we are to live, in relationship to Him, and obeying His Voice.

All of these undergird the mode of the Church as Liberating Army, as all of these modes, focused and sharpened in worship, reveal what a life of liberation is to be, informing us as a Liberating Army exactly what we are to urge people toward to be truly free, as we need all these modal inputs and experiences and Gifts and knowledge to know what it is we are to "disciple all the nations" to be, as we teach them to "obey all the things" Christ has commanded (Matthew 28:19-20). It is in worship we see and hear the paradigm from beyond our history's end revealed in the vision vouchsafed us in worship in the Throne-room of God that is to be remembered and enacted on the earth as a liberating pattern.

So, when Hebrews 10:25 tells us not to forsake the assembling together of ourselves in worship, it's not simply a desire to see high attendance numbers or anything of that sort, but is a Command from the Lord to enter in fellowship with Him and all our brothers to be shaped by what goes on there as He acts by His Word, the Sacraments, the Gifts, and all else involved to shape us into what we already are in Him: the Church marked by and empowered in our various modes of existence to accomplish His Purposes and thus be free.

This is precisely why fishing on a boat by yourself, or sleeping in, or staying home to watch television are *not* what Scripture presents as corporate worship (even if you are having fond feelings for Jesus in those actions). We are to be formed more precisely into what we are called to be in the Presence of the Lord Who walks among His gathered people, and in the midst of our brothers and sisters, rather than as an individualistic "Lone Ranger." We stand or fall as a Redeemed People all together. After all, our destiny is as a people, as we'll see in the next chapter.

CHAPTER 8

WHAT IS OUR DESTINY?

We have seen that we exist as a Romance, a Body, a Family, a Temple, the Ground and Pillar of the Truth, a Weapon, and a Liberating Army. We've seen, as well, that we are not only these things as individuals, but as a collective people. Just as our origin as a people in Christ is a shared one, so our destiny is a shared one in Christ. Attend:

> And He said to them, "Assuredly, I say to you that there are some standing here who will not taste death till they see the kingdom of God present with power." Now after six days Jesus took Peter, James, and John, and led them up on a high mountain apart by themselves; and He was transfigured before them. His clothes became shining, exceedingly white,

like snow, such as no launderer on earth can whiten them. And Elijah appeared to them with Moses, and they were talking with Jesus. Then Peter answered and said to Jesus, "Rabbi, it is good for us to be here; and let us make three tabernacles: one for You, one for Moses, and one for Elijah"— because he did not know what to say, for they were greatly afraid. And a cloud came and overshadowed them; and a voice came out of the cloud, saying, "This is My beloved Son. Hear Him!" Suddenly, when they had looked around, they saw no one anymore, but only Jesus with themselves. Now as they came down from the mountain, He commanded them that they should tell no one the things they had seen, till the Son of Man had risen from the dead. So they kept this word to themselves, questioning what the rising from the dead meant. (Mark 9:1-10, and this historical account is also included in the Gospels of Luke [9: 27-36] and Matthew [17: 1-9].)

What is happening here? What do we read of in this history? What does this mean? The *Transfiguration* is what this is called.

Remember (as the Bible tells us) that Christ Jesus is *both* fully God *and* fully Man, Two Natures in One Person simultaneously. Since the Incarnation, He has *always* been both God and Man (and *still* is). In His Incarnation, the Son subjected Himself to the *Great Kenosis* (the Great Emptying), since "even though He was in the Form of God, He did not consider it robbery to be equal with God," but came "in the likeness of men," becoming "obedient to the point of death, even the Death of the Cross" (Philippians 2:5-11, my translation).

The Eternally Existent Second Person of the Triune God, the Son or Logos, entered the human race by taking to Himself the Perfect Humanity of the Body and Soul engendered on the Virgin Mary by the Holy Spirit, thus becoming, in a Great Mystery, the God-Man, simultaneously both fully God and fully Man.

Philippians 2:8 tells us *why* He did this: He came to die as a Man, thus atoning by the Sacrifice of His Sinless Humanity for the sins of Adam and those descended from him (Romans 5:6-21), and to raise up a redeemed, restored humanity in Himself, thereby becoming the Second Adam (1 Corinthians 15:21-22; 45-49). Those humans who have been born again into the Redeemed, Restored Humanity (John 3:3-8) are grafted into the Very Life, Circumcision, Baptism, Death, Resurrection, Ascension, and Session of the Lord Jesus Christ (Romans 6:1-14; Ephesians 2:1-10: Colossians 2:11-14).

His Life has become *our* life. His Life is *more* important than our life. The Transfiguration account in Mark 9, Luke 9, and Matthew 17 records an event that is an event in which *we*, as members of Christ's Body who have been made part of His Life, *share*. His Transfiguration is *ours*, as well. What, then, does it mean? *The Transfiguration shows us our future destiny.*

Jesus' Transfiguration prefigures that of redeemed human nature, *including* the physical body. This is an important point, since we tend to think like the ancient Gnostic heretics, who pitted "the spiritual" against "the physical," rather than seeing that the Creator has made the physical as the arena for the spiritual, as we see in Christ's Incarnation (He is both Matter and Spirit joined inextricably to the Spiritual Second Person of the Holy Trinity), in the Creation itself (since the physical aspects of the Cosmos, as much as the spiritual aspects, communicate knowledge of the Glories, Nature, Persons, and Attributes of the Spiritual Creator, as Psalm 19:1-6 and Romans 1:18-32 tell us), and as Paul teaches in Romans 12:1-3, where he urges us to present our physical bodies as our "spiritual worship." Salvation is not complete *until* our *bodies* are transfigured, as we'll see. That is the defining mark of our glorification.

Christ's Whole Body was transfigured, becoming the glowing Clothing or Vestment of His Divinity. In this Transfiguration, however, not only His Divine Nature, but also His *Humanity* appeared in Divine Glory.

The Church Fathers of the Seventh Ecumenical Council (787 A.D.) wrote:

"With regard to the nature of the transfiguration, it took place not in such a way that the Word left the human image, but rather in the illumination of this human image by His glory" (6th Session, 12.321 CD).

Jesus here is simply revealing Who He really is, and will be. In His Incarnation, Jesus' Divine Nature is inseparable from His Humanity, even though the Two Natures are united hypostatically, remaining distinct from Each Other, "without mixture or confusion" as the Definition of the Council of Chalcedon (451 A.D.) puts it. In the Transfiguration, the Divine Energies of Jesus' God-Head interpenetrated His Humanity, making His Humanity Resplendent and Luminous by transfiguring It in a Pulse of Uncreated Light.

There on Mount Tabor, Jesus showed us what humanity would be like in Him at the Time of the Restoration of All Things (Acts 3:20-21), also called Doomsday, or the Resurrection of the Dead. 1 John 3:1-3 addresses this time:

Behold what manner of love the Father has bestowed on us, that we should be called children of God! Therefore the world does not know us, because it did not know Him. Beloved, now we are children of God; and it has not yet been revealed what we shall be, but we know that when He is revealed, we shall be like Him, for we shall see Him as He is. And everyone who has this hope in Him purifies himself, just as He is pure.

As does Philippians 3:20-21:

For our citizenship is in heaven, from which we also eagerly wait for the Savior, the Lord Jesus Christ, Who will transform our lowly body that it may be conformed to His Glorious Body, according to the working by which He is able even to subdue all things to Himself.

First Corinthians 15:35-57 also speaks of this:

But someone will say, "How are the dead raised up? And with what body do they come?" Foolish one, what you sow is not made alive unless it dies. And what you sow, you do not sow that body that shall be, but mere grain—perhaps wheat or some other grain. But God gives it a body as He pleases, and to each seed its own body. All flesh is not the same flesh, but there is one kind of flesh of men, another flesh of animals, another of fish, and another of birds. There are also celestial bodies and terrestrial bodies; but the glory of the celestial is one, and the glory of the terrestrial is another. There is one glory of the sun, another glory of the moon, and another glory of the stars; for one star differs from another star in glory. So also is the resurrection of the dead. The body is sown in corruption, it is raised in incorruption. It is sown in dishonor, it is raised in glory. It is sown in weakness, it is raised in power. It is sown a natural body, it is raised a spiritual body. There is a natural body, and there is a spiritual body. And so it is written, "The first man Adam became a living being." The last Adam became a life-giving spirit.

However, the spiritual is not first, but the natural, and afterward the spiritual. The first man was of the earth, made of dust; the second Man is the Lord from heaven. As was the man of dust, so also are those who are made of dust; and as is the heavenly Man, so also are those who are heavenly. And as we have borne the image of the man of dust, we shall also bear the image of the Heavenly Man. Now this I say, brethren, that flesh and blood cannot inherit the kingdom of God; nor does corruption inherit incorruption. Behold, I tell you a mystery: We shall not all sleep, but we shall all be changed— in a moment, in the twinkling of an eye, at the last trumpet. For the trumpet will sound, and the dead will be raised incorruptible, and we shall be changed. For this corruptible must put on incorruption, and this mortal must put on immortality. So when this corruptible has put on incorruption, and this mortal has put on immortality, then shall be brought to pass the saying that is written: "Death is swallowed up in victory." "O Death, where is your sting? O Hades, where is your victory?" The sting of death is sin, and the power of sin is the law. But thanks be to God, who gives us the victory through our Lord Jesus Christ.

These passages all speak to the transfiguration that will take place in us at the Eschaton, the Apotheosis of the Redeemed, when we are changed to be like Him. That will be our *glorification*, when our bodies *and* our spirits will be changed to fully reveal His Glory in us as His Body and Temple.

There is another aspect to this glorification, as well. Genesis 1:26-28 tells us:

> Then God said, "Let Us make man in Our image, according to Our likeness; let them have dominion over the fish of the sea, over the birds of the air, and over the cattle, over all the earth and over every creeping thing that creeps on the earth." So God created man in His Own Image; in the Image of God He created him; male and female He created them. Then God blessed them, and God said to them, "Be fruitful and multiply; fill the earth and subdue it; have dominion over the fish of the sea, over the birds of the air, and over every living thing that moves on the earth."

This passage (as well as Genesis 9:1-3 and the Great Commission of Matthew 28:18-20) teach us that Adam and his descendants were to have the task of dominion over the earth under God. This task involves *glorification*. Adam and his children were to exercise dominion in such a way that the world is changed to make it possible for the created order to achieve its fullest potential, and thus glorify God in the fullest way possible.

Man is himself a microcosm, a small universe or world. He is the center of created life, the means by which God acts in glorifying His Creation. The final goal of Creation is its Transfiguration to fully reveal, on the created level, the Glory of God. Adam failed in this calling when he fell

(Genesis 3), and the Fall's subsequent effects caused his progeny to fail in the task of glorification, as well.

Jesus came into the world as a *Second Adam* (1 Corinthians 15:45-49), atoning for our sins, and producing a redeemed, restored, renewed race of men who *can*, by His Power, fulfill His Original Mandate to take dominion and aid in the glorification of the world. The Second Adam's Task was also Glorification, and, through the Church, He will achieve that goal.

Our proclamation and living out of the Gospel, discipling all the nations to obey all the things He has commanded (Matthew 28:18-20) advances the sanctification and glorification of the world even as the Spirit of Jesus advances *our* sanctification to prepare us for our eventual and sure glorification in Christ.

Not only that, but Romans 8:14-30 says:

> For as many as are led by the Spirit of God, these are sons of God. For you did not receive the spirit of bondage again to fear, but you received the Spirit of adoption by whom we cry out, "Abba, Father." The Spirit Himself bears witness with our spirit that we are children of God, and if children, then heirs—heirs of God and joint heirs with Christ, if indeed we suffer with Him, that we may also be glorified together. For I consider that the sufferings of this present time are not worthy to be compared with the glory which shall be revealed in us. For the earnest expectation of the creation eagerly waits for the revealing of the sons of God. For the

creation was subjected to futility, not willingly, but because of Him Who subjected it in hope; because the creation itself also will be delivered from the bondage of corruption into the glorious liberty of the children of God. For we know that the whole creation groans and labors with birth pangs together until now. Not only that, but we also who have the first fruits of the Spirit, even we ourselves groan within ourselves, eagerly waiting for the adoption, the redemption of our body.

When we are revealed (resurrected and glorified) at the Restoration of All Things (Acts 3:21), the earth itself will be glorified fully, as it is freed from the last vestiges of its bondage to the Prince of Darkness and his perverse world-system.

The earth will be *filled* with the knowledge of the Glory of the Lord, as the waters cover the sea (Habakkuk 2:14), which will bring on the Eschaton, in which there will be a New Heavens and a New Earth (Revelation 21:1; 21:22-22:5), where the physical world, like the bodies of the Redeemed, will be transfigured to fully reflect God's Glory, changed and renewed to be what their intended end has always been.

As we saw back in chapters 6 and 7, we get a glimpse of the New Creation every time we enter Heaven to worship beyond the end of our time in the Shekinah Cloud (Hebrews 12:22-24), and we are to carry this vision before us in the world as a template for the world's transfiguration, a pattern for world-transformation. We see in worship what the world will be. In our vocations and lives, we are to apply God's Word to people, situations and society to see the world transformed by being conformed to Jesus' Image and Will, obeying all the things He has commanded (as Matthew 28:18-20, again, sets out a pattern for the Church's evangelistic and world-renewing vocation).

"Now the Lord is the Spirit; and where the Spirit of the Lord is, there is liberty. But we all, with unveiled face, beholding as in a mirror the glory of the Lord, are being transformed into the same image from glory to glory, just as by the Spirit of the Lord" (2 Corinthians 3:17-18). Just as *we* are being gradually changed in sanctification, so we are to spread the Glory, and, just as Isaiah 28:13 lays out the spread of the influence of God's Word, "Precept upon precept, precept upon precept, line upon line, line upon line, here a little, there a little," and a trickle of water from God's Temple (the Church) becomes a stream, then a river, then a sea that heals all it comes in contact with (Ezekiel 47:1-10), so the advance of God's Kingdom gradually drives back Satan's world-system of darkness, as the Gospel changes men and their cultural and societal constructs.

This is clearly seen in 1 Corinthians 15:20-28, which tells us:

But now Christ is risen from the dead, and has become the firstfruits of those who have fallen asleep. For since by man came death, by Man also came the resurrection of the dead. For as in Adam all die, even so in Christ all shall be made alive. But each one in his own order: Christ the First fruits, afterward those who are Christ's at His Coming. Then comes the end, when He delivers the kingdom to God the Father, when He puts an end to all rule and all authority and power. For He must reign till He has put all enemies under His Feet. The last enemy that will be destroyed is death. For "He has put all things under His feet." But when He says "all things are put under Him," it is evident that He Who put all things under Him is excepted. Now when all things are made subject to Him, then the Son Himself will also be subject to Him Who put all things under Him, that God may be all in all.

This passage tells us clearly "He must reign till He has put all enemies under His Feet" (verse 25), and we know from Ephesians 1:19-22 that God has currently seated Christ at His Right Hand, far above all principality and power, from where He rules all things. The last enemy He will overcome is death (verse 26). Only then will the end come, when He delivers the Kingdom to His Father and puts an end to all rule, authority, and power (verse 24). Until then, He rules from the Father's Right Hand, overcoming His enemies over time until all things are made subject to Him (verse 28).

I realize this somewhat flies in the face of some popular eschatological views which see the Church as only being defeated in history. However, the Church is, as we've seen, the Body of Christ, the Weapon in His Hand, and His Own Spirit-Empowered Liberating Force, one of the vehicles through which Jesus exercises His Expanding Rule as agents of His Kingdom. Regardless of our eschatological position, we should accommodate an optimistic view of what the Lord will accomplish through His People to advance the Rule of His Kingdom. This is very much in line with Jesus' Parables of the Kingdom, where He compares the Kingdom to a mustard seed which grows into a tree in which birds roost (Matthew 13:31-32) and to leaven, which expands, causing bread to rise (Matthew 13:33), examples of growth and enlargement across time. His Kingdom grows across time, and the Church is His Instrument of advance.

Ephesians 1:9-10 tells us History's purpose, and the Call of the Church:

> [H]aving made known to us the mystery of His will, according to His Good Pleasure which He purposed in Himself, that in the dispensation of the fullness of the times He might unite together in one all things in Christ, both which are in heaven and which are on earth—in Him.

God has graciously called us to take our places in His Story, to be used by Jesus to call all things together (in heaven and on earth, as it says). Yet, how can we, who live on the earth, aid in the uniting of things in heaven to those on earth?

Ephesians 3:7-11 explains this:

> ...I became a minister according to the gift of the grace of God given to me by the effective working of His power. To me, who am less than the least of all the saints, this grace was given, that I should preach among the Gentiles the unsearchable riches of Christ, and to make all see what is the fellowship of the mystery, which from the beginning of the ages has been hidden in God Who created all things through Jesus Christ; to the intent that now the Manifold Wisdom of God might be made known by the church to the principalities and powers in the heavenly places, according to the eternal purpose which He accomplished in Christ Jesus our Lord...

It is through the Church that "the Manifold Wisdom of God might be made known...to the principalities and powers in the heavenly places" as God's Purpose of summing up all things in Jesus is seen in, and advanced by, the Church. It is through *us*, the Church, that God's Eternal Purpose is revealed to the powers which will be made subject to Christ, a Goal and Aspect of the Plan which God has designed and prepared to be fulfilled *only* by the Body of Christ, we who are His Redeemed People.

Our destiny as the Church is not only ourselves to be sanctified across our lives and glorified at time's end, but to help advance Christ's Kingdom on the earth, a task which also ties the earth's destiny and renewal to our own. As if this was not enough, we also are the source of revelation to angelic powers by God's Express Will.

What could be more important or fulfilling than this? You are called to preach and live out the Gospel to change the world, and effect eternal, cosmic purposes by your calling and the exercise of your gifts. What more could you want?

To despise this calling is to be Esau, who traded his birthright (leadership over the People of God) for "a mess of pottage," a bowl of soup (Genesis 25:29-34; Hebrews 12:12-17).

Shake yourself and rise from your slumber, and take your place in the Army of the Church, which marches by God's Power to change the world. "Awake, you who sleep; arise from the dead, and Christ will give you light" (Ephesians 5:14).

CHAPTER 9

THE CHURCH AS WHORE

So, we saw in chapter 8 that the Kingdom of God is an expanding, triumphant endeavor as the Gospel is preached and lived out by the Church in the world. However, it's frequently observed that our Western cultures, including America's, are becoming less and less Christian and more and more pagan over the last 70 years or so, leading many people to believe that the end of the world is at hand, expecting the Church to become more and more peripheralized, and for the Church to accomplish less and less. Can this be true?

I mean, it is true that our culture is becoming less and less Christian as time goes on, and our institutions increasingly seek to divest themselves of Biblical norms and understanding. It's also true that, though a huge portion of our population in the United States identify themselves as Christians, the overall percentage *is* shrinking. Why would that be, if indeed the Kingdom will one day advance until the knowledge of the Glory of the Lord covers the earth as the waters cover the seas (Isaiah 11:9; Habakkuk 2:14)?

There are a couple of things we should consider in answering this question. First, the number of Christians in the Third World (Asia, Africa, and South America) has been steadily and exponentially increasing across the last century, and Christianity is now the largest religious faith in the world (and still accelerating) because of that expanse. In terms of overall global presence, the Kingdom is aggressively expanding.

However, here in the West, which was largely built and shaped by Biblical principles and ethics, the Church seems to be shrinking; why is that?

Consider the following account from 2 Chronicles 7:12-14:

> Then the LORD appeared to Solomon by night, and said to him: "I have heard your prayer, and have chosen this place for Myself as a house of sacrifice. When I shut up heaven and there is no rain, or command the locusts to devour the land, or send pestilence among My people, if My People who are called by My name will humble themselves, and pray and

153

seek My face, and turn from their wicked ways, then I will
hear from heaven, and will forgive their sin and heal their
land.

This occurred right after Solomon finished building
the Temple. Is this not an odd thing to say, especially at
the dedication of the Temple? What is behind God telling
Solomon this? Why would God say such a thing?

The Lord says when He "shuts up Heaven and there
is no rain," or commands "the locusts to devour the land"
(eating up their food), or sends "pestilence (sickness)"
among His People, and you'll note that He says "*when*" I
do these things, not "*if*" but *when* I do these things, *then*
"if My People who are called by My Name will humble
themselves and pray, etc., etc...." The question turns on the
context of the Divine Statement. What is the context? Why
did God say this to Solomon, and, through Him, to us?

The context here is most odd to most of us, because
surely God wouldn't withhold rain, send locusts to devour
the fields, or send pestilence among His *Own* People,
would he? Well, in a word, *yes*, He would. Though God is
most Merciful, He is also Just, and He is not *more* Merciful
than He is Just. His Attributes are equally ultimate, as the
theologians would say. While God *is* Merciful beyond
our ability to count or say, it is also true that He *hates*
sin, because He is Holy, and will not even *look* upon sin
(Leviticus 19:2; Psalm 99; Habakkuk 1:13), and Scripture

tells us that God sets a limit on the iniquities that He will allow a culture to have (pagan *or* covenanted; Genesis 15:13-16).

Though God *is* Long-suffering and Patient, His Hatred of evil and Love for righteousness motivate Him to set a line beyond which He will not allow a people to rack up iniquity beyond, without that filling-up of the quota of sin triggering God's Actions in Judgment against that nation. So, yes, God does judge His People (as He does all nations, including His Multi-national Nation of kings and priests, the Church, cf. 1 Peter 2:9; 1 Corinthians 5:1-5; 11:27-32; Acts 5:1-11).

Why would God say this to the Church? We saw in earlier chapters that we worship in Heaven, and carry the vision of that before us as a template to inform the building of the Kingdom, and that our evangelism is to aim at the discipleship of *all* areas of life, both personal and communal (a cultural revolution), to obedience to all that Christ has commanded us, which shows us that culture flows from cult (so that what we believe controls what we do). What we *worship* is what we *become* like. We *act out* the values of what we worship throughout our lives, outside of the place in which we formally and fully worship.

If the time comes when God looks at a nation and thinks it so sinful He must discipline it, it would be because He would judge that that nation is not living up to

His Will. You see this all over the Bible. My cursory count in Isaiah alone revealed fourteen nations God promised to judge for just what we're talking about here (and that doesn't even take into account Ezekiel, Daniel, Habakkuk, the other Prophets, or the Law).

Here's the deal: God is not playing. This life and Creation of His are not a game to Him. He hates sin, He loves His People, and He has a Purpose, which is to make His People holy as He is Holy, and for His Holy People, the Church, to help make the world around them into the sort of place God designed and intended it to be: a place for His Worship, structured according to His Word, where His Glory is as fully revealed as it can possibly be by created things.

If a nation refuses to be that kind of place, the question is: Why? There are a couple of possibilities: First, there are a number of nations on the face of the earth which simply don't have many Christians there yet. The Gospel is just being preached in those places, the Church is relatively new there and is, in many ways, in its infancy in those places. This situation exists in Asia and some parts of Africa, for instance. However, in most countries today, there is a sizeable number of Christians, and, anywhere where the Church is, *if* the Church is doing what it should be doing, it will change that country.

How do I know this? Because culture comes from *cult*, from worship. Christians go into Heaven to worship, and see a vision of the world to come, illuminated by the Living Word, and then the Church, God's Weapon and Liberating Army, the Ground and Pillar of His Truth, is to come back from the Heavenly Liturgy in the Heavenly Tabernacle (Hebrews 12:22-24), with the Vision of God before their eyes, and the Word of God upon their lips and in their hearts, and they go to live these things out in the world.

People see this in the Christian's lives, and hear the Gospel preached by the Church, and they join us, and then *they* do the same things as the Church, and the nation changes as it progressively embodies the Commands of Christ in its life and culture. That's what happened in Europe and America, and it is what is now happening in Asia and the Global South. The Gospel changes the world. This pleases God. This is the job, the *raison d'être*, the reason for being of the Church.

Keeping these things in mind, let us turn to Matthew 5:13-16:

You are the salt of the earth; but if the salt loses its flavor, how shall it be seasoned? It is then good for nothing but to be thrown out and trampled underfoot by men. You are the light of the world. A city that is set on a hill cannot be hidden. Nor do they light a lamp and put it under a basket, but on a lamp stand, and it gives light to all who are in the house. Let your light so shine before men, that they may see your good works and glorify your Father in heaven.

Here Jesus calls the Church salt and light. What does salt do? It flavors things, of course, which is the way most Westerners think of it, and, of course, it does that very well. In cultures where they don't have refrigeration, however, salt performs another very important function: it *preserves* things, and keeps them from rotting and becoming rank and useless (things like meat, for instance). This is primarily the sense in which Jesus is referring to the Church as "salt," since the Church's lived and preached Gospel flavors and preserves the worthwhile parts of life.

This same Church is also the light of the world; we are the light-bearers of the Light of Christ, a veritable City lit from within by the Light of the Lamb of God. The light of the Gospel carried forward by the Church drives back the darkness and holds it at bay, while the salt of the Church flavors and preserves what replaces the darkness.

So how *are* we to be salt and light to the world? Well, consider what Jesus goes on to say in the following verses in Matthew 5:17-20 (ESV; NKJV, yes, together):

Do not think that I have come to abolish the Law or the Prophets; I have not come to abolish them but to fulfill them. For assuredly, I say to you, till heaven and earth pass away, one jot or one tittle will by no means pass from the law till all is fulfilled. Whoever therefore breaks one of the least of these commandments, and teaches men so, shall be called least in the kingdom of heaven; but whoever does and teaches them, he shall be called great in the kingdom of heaven. For I say to you, that unless your righteousness exceeds the righteousness of the scribes and Pharisees, you will by no means enter the kingdom of heaven.

How to be salt and light? Do what Jesus has said. Do His Book. Keep His Word. Living His Word out, *really* living it, is part of His Story, the Story that we were created to take part in.

The Pharisees *seemed* to live out God's Word, but they only *seemed* to; they actually *didn't* live it out at all. Jesus said they looked good, but that they were full of dead men's bones, like tombs (Matthew 23:27). What Jesus was saying is that, if His Word truly permeates you, and you walk in terms of His Word, then you *will* be light to the darkness, and salt to preserve that which should be preserved.

However, in verse 13 of Matthew 5, Jesus asks what should be done about the salt that has lost its flavor; it's not good, He says, for anything. It won't preserve or taste good—not good for *anything*. Verses 15 and 16 record Jesus warning us against *hiding* our light. Hide the light, He said, and the darkness returns to dominate that place. As the Church, we are a Weapon and a Liberating Force. This means we are at *war*. We're all soldiers. We have an enemy, and at war people are wounded, hurt, maimed, and killed. There is no quarter given between Satan and God.

Why would salt lose its savor, or the lights be hidden? Why would the Church *do* that? Well, we've seen that the Church is the Romance of God, the Bride of Christ (Revelation 21:2, 9; 22:17). The Old Covenant Church of Israel is frequently referred to by the Prophets as the Bride or Wife of YHWH (Isaiah 54:5-6; Jeremiah 3:14, 20; Hosea 2:2). Whenever the Church, Old or New Covenant, begins to pursue other gods, it's called spiritual *whoredom*.

Now, we don't get too many sermons on this subject these days. But even though it's tellingly, largely ignored in the pulpit today, we all know what a whore is. It's an ugly word for an ugly thing. A whore is a person who engages in sexual intercourse outside of marriage (which is the *only* legitimate setting for sexual intercourse) in exchange for money or favors of some sort. (Sometimes we call a whore a prostitute these days.) Sex is only for marriage. A whore ignores what is right in that regard.

God describes the behavior of the Church, whenever she walks away from what is right to do to get favors by worshipping other gods as spiritual *whoredom*, with all its attendant diseases and filth. Strong words. Ezekiel 16:1-3, 14-43 records a number of incredibly disturbing things that God was saying to His Bride, Israel:

> Again the word of the LORD came to me, saying, "Son of man, cause Jerusalem to know her abominations," and say, 'Thus says the Lord GOD to Jerusalem: "Your birth and your nativity are from the land of Canaan; your father was an Amorite and your mother a Hittite...Your fame went out among the nations because of your beauty, for it was perfect

through My splendor which I had bestowed on you," says the Lord GOD. "But you trusted in your own beauty, played the harlot because of your fame, and poured out your harlotry on everyone passing by who would have it. You took some of your garments and adorned multicolored high places for yourself, and played the harlot on them. Such things should not happen, nor be. You also took your beautiful jewels of my gold and of my silver, which I had given you, and made for yourself images of men, and with them played the whore. You took your embroidered garments and covered them, and you set My Oil and My Incense before them. Also My Food which I gave you—the pastry of fine flour, oil, and honey which I fed you— you set it before them as sweet incense; and so it was," says the Lord GOD. "Moreover you took your sons and your daughters, whom you bore to Me, and these you sacrificed to them to be devoured. Were your acts of harlotry a small matter, that you have slain My Children and offered them up to them by causing them to pass through the fire? And in all your abominations and acts of harlotry you did not remember the days of your youth, when you were naked and bare, struggling in your blood. Then it was so, after all your wickedness—'Woe, woe to you!' says the Lord GOD—"that you also built for yourself a shrine, and made a high place for yourself in every street. You built your high places at the head of every road, and made your beauty to be abhorred. You offered yourself to everyone who passed by, and multiplied your acts of harlotry. You also committed harlotry with the Egyptians, your very fleshly neighbors, and increased your acts of harlotry to provoke Me to anger.

Behold, therefore, I stretched out My hand against you, diminished your allotment, and gave you up to the will of those who hate you, the daughters of the Philistines, who were ashamed of your lewd behavior. You also played the harlot with the Assyrians, because you were insatiable; indeed you played the harlot with them and still were not satisfied. You multiplied your whoring also with the trading land of Chaldea, and even with this you were not satisfied. How degenerate is your heart!" says the Lord GOD, "seeing you do all these things, the deeds of a brazen harlot. You erected your shrine at the head of every road, and built your high place in every street. Yet you were not like a harlot, because you scorned payment. You are an adulterous wife, who takes strangers instead of her husband. Men give gifts to all prostitutes, but you gave your gifts to all your lovers, bribing them to come to you from every side with your whorings. So you were different from other women in your whorings. No one solicited you to play the whore, and you gave payment, while no payment was given to you; therefore you were different. Now then, O harlot, hear the Word of the LORD! Thus says the Lord GOD, Because your lust was poured out and your nakedness uncovered in your whorings with your lovers, and with all your abominable idols, and because of the blood of your children that you gave to them, surely, therefore, I will gather all your lovers with whom you took pleasure, all those you loved, and all those you hated; I will gather them from all around against you and will uncover your nakedness to them, that they may see all your nakedness. And I will judge you as women who brewed lock or shed blood are judged; I will bring blood upon you in fury and jealousy. I will also give you into their hand, and they shall throw down your shrines and break down your high places. They shall also strip you of your clothes, take your beautiful jewelry, and leave you naked and bare. They shall also bring up an assembly against you, and they shall stone you with stones and thrust you through with their swords. And they shall burn your houses and execute judgments upon you in the sight of many women. I will make you stop playing the whore, and you shall also give payment no more. So I will lay to rest My Fury toward you, and My Jealousy shall depart from you. I will be quiet, and be angry no more. Because you did not remember the days of your youth, but agitated Me with all these things, surely I will also recompense your deeds on your own head," says the Lord GOD.'

God is saying here, "You've gone off after all these other gods; you've erected shrines to these false gods; you've gone out in all your perverse lusts after those pagan nations, and not only did you *not* take money for these things like a normal whore would, but you paid *them*!!"

The Lord was *angry* here. He accused His Bride, "You make your children pass through the fire!" (a form of pagan child-sacrifice to their dark gods). Israel, God's Bride, had turned from pure worship of Him to other alien gods, and, in search of fertility and prosperity, were sacrificing their children in the flames. In the Old Testament, over and over again, God tells Israel, "Your children are Mine!" (Ezekiel 16:8, 21, 36; *cf.* Isaiah 1:2; 4; 43:1; 63:8; Jeremiah 30:20; 49:11; Ezekiel 18:4; 23:4-5; Malachi 3:17). These Israelites were giving *His* Covenanted Children to pagan gods. The Lord was mightily and deservedly *hacked.*

In response, God said, "I'm going to subject you to all manner of Judgments. I found you deserted, and I fed, clothed, washed, and, when you were old enough, I married you, and then, even though you were my wife, you turned around and ran after these pagan gods. Basically, I've had enough—I've had *enough!*"

Now, some of you may be saying, "O.K., Kemper, but this is 21st-Century America. We don't worship pagan gods here. No Ashteroth or Baalim or Moloch here, like the gods they used to worship back then." Well, that's *sort* of true. We don't worship Moloch and Baal here, at least *not under those names.* We worship gods of other names here, because, in this increasingly post-Christian society, the true names of the old gods are anathema.

Nonetheless, the impulses and desires that drove the worship of those idols are still very much with us in the postmodern West, driving much of our contemporary worship. We've simply given the ancient gods new, modern, socially-acceptable *names*, while the demonic powers behind those old gods are plenty happy to change the old masks for ones acceptable to post-Enlightenment reductionists. The worship, you see, is still the same, having the same effects, yielding the same spiritual destruction among the all-too-frequently unsuspecting worshippers of the new/old dark and bloody gods.

The sophisticated new names of the gods, you ask? Well, they're names like Commerce (used to be called Mammon), Security and Power, Creature Comforts, and, of course, Pleasure. All of these categories, in their places and proper usages, are acceptable and good concepts, servants of the good. But when we see these things as the primary means by which we are to be fulfilled and made happy, they become idols, and we begin to bend our lives to their service, sacrificing more and more so that our lives will be shaped by those things, and the worship of the Triune God becomes more and more peripheral, forced to one side, so that we can serve the gods we *really* love.

The Israelites of Ezekiel 16 still had the Temple and the Scriptures, the Priesthood and the Sacrifices all going on, yet a huge portion of the nation was worshipping the pagan gods off to the side in the darkness. Going through the motions does not make a person a worshipper of God. So much of the American Church today is all caught up in the adoration of these same false gods.

We have a nation with 65-70 million people claiming to be born-again Christians. That's a substantial portion of our population. That's a *lot* of people. However, we live in a country where our schools, by governmental decree, will not teach you that there is a Creator (even though it's in our Founding Documents...), and where over fifty percent of our marriages end in divorce (serial polygamy, anyone?), and where 4000 unborn Americans a day are murdered (to facilitate convenience, economic ease, and to avoid the consequences of [generally illicit] sexual activity, activity which the government *protects*), I personally don't see any difference between that and sacrificing your baby in the fire to Moloch, (especially since the sacrifices to Moloch were for much the same reasons).

All this is going on with 70 million self-proclaimed Christians in our society. If *half* that number were being the salt and light they are supposed to be, (1) there'd be a *lot* more Christians here, and (2) the salt they were and the light they'd shed would halt the deterioration and drive back the advance of the darkness of many evil practices. But that's *not* really happening at present. Why is that?

You can turn to Deuteronomy Chapter 28 to see how God assesses this type of situation in a covenantal way. "If you (the collective nation) obey," He says, "I'll shower these blessings on you and your society" (Deuteronomy 28:1-13). Conversely, "If you (the collective people) *disobey* My Word," He says later in the chapter," I will bring wave after wave of judgment on you, each successive wave escalating in severity and impact, until, as a people, you either repent or are destroyed (Deuteronomy 28:14-68, a much *longer* list than that of the blessings...). Each wave of judgment is an opportunity to repent.

If you know much about America's history of late, you can read our recent history as a nation in the latter portion of Deuteronomy 28 (also in Leviticus 26:14-39). Our early history parallels the earlier blessing part of the chapter. But our history over the last 50—60 years can be read in the cursing or judgment part of the chapter in an uncannily accurate recapitulation of those waves of judgment. You can see where we are on that spectrum, and, very scarily, we are much farther along the judgment process than any of us really want to believe.

Once upon a time, we were a people who predominantly loved the Triune God, and built our institutions and lives in accordance with Christ's Word. Increasingly, despite a large presence of professing Christians here, our nation continues to self-consciously and gradually depart from the Biblical Norms for how we should live as a nation. Why *is* that?

It's because the Church in America (not all of it, but many portions of it) have gone whoring after strange gods. That is distressing, don't you think? It distresses me, because I can read Ezekiel 16, Leviticus 24, and Deuteronomy 28, and see our history opening up before my eyes. In my lifetime, I have seen America progressively turning away from God, and that departure is steadily escalating (Europe is far ahead of us, by the way, but we are working hard to catch them up, it appears). What will our state as a nation be 20—40 years hence? Think we'll survive at all? When do *you* think our iniquity will be full, and our sin-quota complete?

Here's the deal. *The key to everything,* both in this country and in all countries across the world, *is what the Church does.* Not what the pagans do, but what the *Church* does.

Well, Kemper, you say, I don't believe in abortion or divorce or stuff like that. Why would *I* be in trouble for our nation doing those things? Because the Church's job is to walk out into the world around us and be salt and light to the culture, and the Church in America today (to which all we American Christians belong) has *not* done that.

We're comfortable sitting in our churches Sunday by Sunday, being taught, soaking it all up, and feeling really good about ourselves, learning about Jesus, and going home to wait for the Rapture, thinking it's all going to be all right when the rest of the country goes to Hell on a handrail. The problem with this is that we, the Church, have a responsibility together to be the priests of the earth, representing God to man and man to God in our culture. *We* are responsible to be God's Liberating Army, His Weapon against the dark kingdom. *We* are responsible to be salt and light to our community and to the world.

We have met the enemy, and he is *us*. We're much more interested in football than we are in prayer. We're much more interested in television series than we are in Bible study. We're sure as heck more interested in not embarrassing ourselves publicly than we are in sharing the Gospel with someone. Do you smell the whiff of incense burned to dark gods in those behaviors? We like to be entertained, and comfortable, and satisfied, and feel good, and we think that by going to church on Sunday that we're being salt and light, when we are *not* doing so. The Church is changing other cultures in other countries across the world, but it's not happening in America anymore, except sporadically in small areas for short bursts of time. This is why, though the Kingdom is currently advancing in other parts of the world, it isn't here in America and the West. We're under judgment here.

Why have I written all these hard truths down (and talked about it across the country), taking the time and preparation to prepare this book? Because if we don't, as a people, live out these things we've learned, we're done for. We're dog-meat in the good old U.S. of A., and I'm not even exaggerating one little bit. Done for. I haven't written all this down to tell platitudes to make us all feel good. We need to *live out* these things. It is our duty and our destiny to do so. It is our privilege and freedom to do so. It is our part in God's Great Story.

It is a right and necessary thing to do. If the Church does not wake up and start *being* the Church, this country will continue to go down into the darkness. Read the end of the judgment process in Deuteronomy 28, and you will see our likely history writ large. We're in bad shape. No question about it. So is there hope? Of course there is.

What is the passage we read at this chapter's beginning? Second Chronicles 7:14 tells us that if the Nation of Priests repent and seek God and begin to live as the Church, God promises to *heal* their land. If the Weapon that the Church is would be sharpened, if the Liberating Army that we are would actually leave their barracks and go forth to make war, there is hope for us. There is hope if the Church repents. If it doesn't, though, there is *no* hope.

Understand that. Understand that we Christians have an opportunity to do something substantive to change the situation. If we fail, we are *done for* as a people. That is *truth*. Life is structured by God's Covenant, and God has put you here for just such a time as this (as Mordecai told Esther in Esther 4:14). This is truth, and it'll give you the power to do the right thing. There were 120 people in the Upper Room at Pentecost when the Holy Spirit fell (Acts chapters 1 and 2), and those few people changed the entire world. There are a great many more people than that who are believers in our day, and I'd actually settle for half the world. Do you think that's possible?

It's happened before, and it can happen again. If we will be the Church, we'll change everything in this country, in this hemisphere, in the world. And we'll be the Bridge of Truth and Glory into the future, as we become what we were born to be. Let us rouse ourselves, and be who we are supposed to be now in this time. This is God's Will for us all.

CHAPTER 10

LIBERATION FRONT

Romance. Body. Family. Temple. Pillar and Ground of the Truth. Weapon. Liberating Army. These are the primary modes of existence we've seen in this book which define and describe us as the Church, modes of existence which are paths of freedom for the People of God and the world in which we live. In the last chapter, we saw that our culture is in deep trouble, and that only the Church, empowered and directed by God, can bring about a renewal and resurgence in our country—a liberation.

How should we think about liberating our societies? Scripture provides a paradigm for us to understand and engage the culture around us in its account of the Sons of Issachar in 1 Chronicles 12:32: "...of the sons of Issachar who had understanding of the times, to know what Israel ought to do...."

The Tribe of Issachar joined the Israelite forces under King David who came "to turn over the kingdom of Saul to him according to the Word of The Lord" (1 Chronicles 12:23) after Saul and his dynasty's tragic end on Mount Gilboa (1 Chronicles 10). As the Bible says, they knew what their Tribe should do since they understood their national situation.

This is a two-fold thrust by the Sons of Issachar: first, they "understood the times," e.g., they carefully worked to correctly discern the history, culture, politics, religious climate, and so forth, of their place in time, which is to say, they didn't just make a snap judgment based on a guess or feeling about their current situation (and they didn't have talking-head media pundits to supposedly analyze and "sum it all up" [more like "dumb it all down"] for them). They had to think hard and pay close attention to how the events of their time had developed, the factors and reasons that the situations they faced had unfolded in the way they were.

No situation we face in this world just suddenly sprang into being. Our history is a continuum, with preceding events, cultural developments, and societal attitudes contributing (either positively or negatively) to those of the present. In the situation of the Issacharians mentioned in 1 Chronicles 12:32, they had to not only know about, but also understand how the dynastic origins, triumphs, and failings of King Saul had unfolded, the attitudes and political leanings of the other Tribes of Israel, their own Tribe's interactions, influence, and possible conflicts with the other Tribes (not to mention any inter-tribal conflicts in their own Tribe), the threat and possible advantages of the views of the nations (both allies and enemies) round about Israel as to the establishment of a new Davidic Dynasty, the resources required (and the risk to those resources involved) in support or resistance to a Davidic take-over of the reigns of civil government in Israel, the history of David and his family and Tribe (which would likely enjoy favored status in ways as the Tribe of the king), the leanings of the military in the situation, the threat and possibilities of military action or war in Israel or internationally in establishing David as king, etc., etc.

This was, obviously, a complicated question, with nuanced evaluations across a broad scale necessary to their understanding of the times. This was the *horizontal* dimension of their understanding, the bare facts, as it were. It was still, however, necessary to be able to accurately assess the *meaning* and appropriateness of that data. These facts were the *is*, but the Sons of Issachar had to arrive at an *ought* for their nation. This leads us to the second prong of the two-fold thrust of "understanding the times to know what Israel should do." That "should" in this verse is what amounts to an "ought;" this is a *moral* question, a question of right versus wrong behavior, a question which requires a guide or standard. For ancient Israel, as for the

Church today, that guide and standard can only be the Scriptures, the Word of God, which, as the Written Word of the Incarnate and Divine Word, the Lord Jesus, tells us how we *ought* to live, and is the Standard of our lives and morality (2 Timothy 3:16-17; 2 Peter 1:19-21), a truth driven home by the words of Hebrews 4:12-13:

> For the word of God is living and powerful, and sharper than any two-edged sword, piercing even to the division of soul and spirit, and of joints and marrow, and is a discerner of the thoughts and intents of the heart. And there is no creature hidden from His sight, but all things are naked and open to the eyes of Him to whom we must give account.

There is nothing hidden from the Lord, and He Who sees all things, even to the spiritual and physical differences, and the thoughts and intents of an individual's heart, also sees the collective intent and will of a people, assessing these exposed elements, and speaking authoritatively to the entire experience, desires, and plans of both individuals and peoples, as we've seen previously (the reason why we are to "disciple all the nations...teaching them to obey everything..." Christ has commanded (Matthew 28:19-20). The Bible is our Standard, a fact not lost upon the Sons of Issachar.

It is only through God's Word that we are able to assess facts (of history or anything else) as to their meaning in God's Will and Plan, and thus to our moral course of action (what we *should* or *ought to* do) in light of the meaning of those facts (the great Christian theologian/philosopher Cornelius Van Til was wont to say, "There is no brute factuality," by which he meant that all created things, whatever their category, exist with an already attached set of meanings given them by the Creator, and men were not free to simply attach other meanings generated by their own Fallen desires and sinful concepts; the Bible is the source to which we must look to "think God's Thoughts after Him" and thus assess facts correctly).

The reason the Sons of Issachar were able to "understand the times" is that they correctly assessed the facts of their situation in light of what Scripture said. They knew the Word of God (and doubtless were aware of Samuel's anointing of David; cf. 1 Samuel 16:1-13), and were thereby able to understand the meaning of the events of their time, and thus "to know what Israel should do," an ethical insight born of seeing the events of their time by the illumination of the Biblical Standard. You'll note that the Sons of Issachar didn't just know what the Tribe of Issachar was supposed to do, but what "Israel," *all* the Tribes of the nation, should do. They were able to draw universal conclusions concerning the ethical demands of all the People of God by their Biblical understanding of their times. This is the *vertical* dimension of their understanding the times and knowing what Israel should do, the insight and interpretive advantage won in any situation by being able to assess the events of life in terms of what God's Word says, a spiritual insight that the Bible calls *wisdom*, a necessary insight, if the Church is going to be what it should be, and do what it is called to do.

This should, again, fill us with determination to learn and deeply absorb the Bible, so we can consistently apply its standards and teachings to the events of our lives and of those around us, and is, of course, a vital aspect of our being the Pillar and Ground of the Truth, and the Liberating Force God has called us to be. If we are to function in our own time as Sons of Issachar, we too must learn to carefully assess the world around us by looking, as Saint John Calvin said, through the "lenses of Scripture" to correct our sin-distorted vision, accurately consider the facts around us, and know what should be done to fulfill the Will of God.

The implications of the account of the Sons of Issachar as a paradigm for the Church are many, but one implication sticks out amongst the myriad: Belief leads to action. Theory (*theoria*) informs practice (*practicum*), e.g., ideas have consequences. Our belief, theory, ideas will inform our action, practice, and consequences, and we therefore must make certain that our theory and beliefs are founded upon the Revelation of God's Word, or our resultant actions will not only not accomplish what they should be accomplishing, but may be harmful or catastrophic (kind of like, ummmm, much of what the Church has been doing over the last half a century or so).

There is an interrelated, interpenetrative order to the foundational aspect of the seven modes of the Church we've been looking at in this book, an order which flows from belief to action in informing who we are and what we are to do as the Church, which, if embraced, will fit us to become Sons and Daughters of Issachar for our time. The following lays that out for us.

First, FOUNDATION or BELIEF or THEORIA:

Romance

It is necessary that we first have a relationship with the Living God, that we *know* Him (Jeremiah 31:34; Hosea 6:3; 2 Timothy 1:12; 1 John 2:3-5). We must know and *love* the Lord (Deuteronomy 6:5; Matthew 22:37; Mark 12:30; Luke 10:27), just as He has *loved* us (Deuteronomy 7:13; Jeremiah 31:3; Hosea 14:4; Zephaniah 3:17; John 3:16; 13:34; 14:23; 15:9-10; Romans 5:5-8; 8:35-39; Ephesians 2:14; 3:19; 5:25; 1 John 4:12-19). We must know God *experientially*, to have an ongoing experience with Him, supported by, and giving rise to A DISCIPLINED LIFE.

Temple

WORSHIP: Our experience of the Lord is to be grounded in our worship: personal (daily prayer and study of His Word), familial (drawing our family members into a relationship with Christ), and corporate (offering ourselves to Him with a sacrifice of praise, covenantally re-affirming our relationship with God through the Sacraments, hearing His Word to establish vision, and receiving the benefit of the Spirit's Gifts to the Body, developing networks of support, mutual interest, and ministry). Resources such as the Book of Common Prayer and the Daily Office can help organize and focus our worship in all these areas.

PRAYER: While we normally think of prayer as a petition—that is, making our needs known to God, we should also realize that prayer is to be relational, flowing from our relationship with God, a two-way communication in which we are to listen for and heed the Lord's Communication to us (Genesis 18:20-33; John 16:13; Romans 8:26), which not only provides long-term guidance for us, but the intimacy of real relationship and short-term guidance, as well. This is also incredibly helpful when we engage (as we should, as 1 Timothy 2:1, 8; 1 Peter 4:7; Revelation 5:8; James 5:16, as Jesus also modeled for us, as Matthew 14:23; Mark 6:46; Luke 6:12; 9:28; and 10:2) in intercession for all men (1 Timothy 2:1). All of this is also to be informed and shaped by

Temple and Pillar and Ground of the Truth

SCRIPTURE: It is the Bible that provides the parameters of our ethical behavior—in worship, businesses, relationships, and everything else—since it is the Word of God breathed by the Holy Spirit (2 Timothy 3:16-17) given to provide guidance in every situation of life (2 Peter 1:19-21; Isaiah 8:20). We are not just to possess the knowledge mediated by the Scriptures, but are also to *continue* in the Word, letting it soak into every area of our lives and make us disciples, so we can be free through knowing and living in the Truth (John 8:31-36). The Bible, by the Grace of God, provides believers with a Divine Paradigm, a mind-set-forming Map of Reality. Saint. John Calvin called Scripture the Lens of Scripture which corrects our sin-distorted vision as we gaze through it at the world. As Proverbs 3:5-6 tells us: "Trust in the LORD with all your heart, And lean not on your own understanding; In all your ways acknowledge Him, and He shall direct your paths." We are to trust to His Providential Plan (a relational aspect) and His Knowledge (acknowledging His Purposes, Assessments, and Will in everything we do). This Scripture-saturated life gives rise to

Body and Family

FELLOWSHIP: We are to live our lives *together*, as a community of believers, with accountability to each other, including our friends (Ephesians 5:21), to the leaders Christ has appointed over His People (Hebrews 13:17); to our parents (Ephesians 6:1-4; Colossians 3:20); to our mates

(Ephesians 5:22-33; 1 Peter 3:1-7), and civil magistrates (Romans 13:1-7; Titus 3:1). These relationships are meant to promote discipleship among the Body (both generally for all believers and specifically for particular callings within God's Body), and God provides spiritual directors in *both* these categories, as someone more mature in the calling helps us to grow and be more effective in our ministries. Corporate fellowship exposes us to the exercise of the Gifts of the Spirit distributed among the fellow members of God's Family (1 Corinthians 12:1-31; Romans 12:4-8), providing edification and help for the whole Body of Christ).

These aspects of the foundation, belief, or *theoria* give rise to ACTION, SUPERSTRUCTURE, or *PRACTICUM*.

Liberating Force and Weapon

Matthew 5:13-16, as we've seen, tells us to be salt and light to the world, to scatter the darkness and preserve the effects of the light, flavoring life.

This twofold action is embodied through

WITNESS: The Great Commission of Matthew 28:18-20 shows us that *discipleship* is the core and goal of our outreach, as we disciple all the nations to teach them "to obey all the things I have commanded you" (verse 20), seeing conversion as a starting-point for believers. This witness is to be more than just words; as Saint. Francis taught, "Preach the Gospel always. Use words if necessary," which addresses the necessity of living life consistently as a *context* for the Gospel (as Marshall McLuhan had it, the medium is the message), which means, among other things, *doing our jobs well,* as just such a context, showing the importance of

VOCATION: Vocation or Calling must be understood in Light of Scripture's teaching, as our callings in Christ must be thought through and considered illuminated by Biblical teaching—what our callings mean in light of God's Overall Plan, and how to do them well as God intends and demands. *Everything* is addressed in Scripture in precept, principle, or example (or all three), as the Bible equips believers to be thoroughly "equipped for every good work" (2 Timothy 3:16-17), which necessarily includes everything God might call us to (and thus, all our potential callings).

DOMINION THROUGH SERVICE: Matthew 20:25-28 tells us:

> But Jesus called them to Himself and said, "You know that the rulers of the Gentiles lord it over them, and those who are great exercise authority over them. Yet it shall not be so among you; but whoever desires to become great among you, let him be your servant. And whoever desires to be first among you, let him be your slave—just as the Son of Man did not come to be served, but to serve, and to give His life a ransom for many."

Unlike the pagans, our service to others is to image out and advance the Rule of Christ among His People (and, consequently, in the world). We are to pour ourselves into people. By doing so, we are to do what is good, and show the Kingdom by living it out to others. We are to serve one another by speaking the truth in love (Ephesians 4:15), a service which has dire consequences if it is carried out in imbalance: if we speak the truth without love, it produces a legalistic model of the Faith, and if we speak untruth in love, it produces a sentimental model of the Faith (and both forms have found fertile roots in the American Church). Both truth and love, *together*, are necessary to provide a healthy and balanced Biblical expression of Christianity in the Church.

WARFARE: Luke 12:49-53 lays out the shape of the effects of following Jesus:

"I came to send fire on the earth, and how I wish it were already kindled! But I have a baptism to be baptized with, and how distressed I am till it is accomplished! Do you suppose that I came to give peace on earth? I tell you, not at all, but rather division. For from now on five in one house will be divided: three against two, and two against three. Father will be divided against son and son against father, mother against daughter and daughter against mother, mother-in-law against her daughter-in-law and daughter-in-law against her mother-in-law."

In this Fallen world, the In-breaking and Expanse of the Kingdom of God inevitably generate resistance, since there is no final victory over the world-system (the part of the world still under the rule of Satan, cf. John 12:31; 16:11; 2 Corinthians 4:4; 1 John 5:19) until the Lord returns, even though He has already overcome the Devil in principle, as 1 John 5:4 tells us (and the world-system is steadily passing away before the advance of Christ's Kingdom, as 1 Corinthians 7:31 tells us). There is still ongoing conflict, of course, until that victory is made complete. As if that weren't enough, all believers are still locked in internal conflict with our old natures, the part of us that is at war with the Spirit's Sanctification of His People (Romans 7:17-25; 8:3-4; Ephesians 4:17-27), which has been crucified with Christ (Romans 6:1-10), though it still continues to struggle until our physical death takes place. Christ Jesus *has* overcome the world-system of Satan, and He gives us the ability to not fulfill the lusts and temptations of our old natures by walking in the Filling of the Spirit (Galatians 5:16-18; Ephesians 5:18), but, until these final fulfillments are accomplished in actuality, we are still at war. So, conflict will envelope all of us until Doomsday. Like the Lord Jesus, we are to devote all of our lives and time to making war on the darkness, as His Empowered Weapon and Liberating Army. As Jesus told us in Luke 12, division and fire and pain are necessary to bring healing to our Fallen world.

We must be poured out like drink-offerings before the Lord (2 Timothy 4:6) as living sacrifices (Romans 12:1-2). The heart, the very core of Christianity is ethics driven by sacrificial love. Our attitude must be that of Esther before she risked her life by appearing before the Emperor unannounced, when she told Mordecai, "If I perish, I perish" (Esther 4:16), or of Job in the midst of his sufferings, when he said, "Though He slay me, yet will I trust in Him" (Job 13:15).

Being the Church is not a game; Jesus warned us about this in Luke 14:26-35:

> If anyone comes to Me and does not hate his father and mother, wife and children, brothers and sisters, yes, and his own life also, he cannot be My disciple. And whoever does not bear his cross and come after Me cannot be My disciple. For which of you, intending to build a tower, does not sit down first and count the cost, whether he has enough to finish it— lest, after he has laid the foundation, and is not able to finish, all who see it begin to mock him, saying, 'This man began to build and was not able to finish.' Or what king, going to make war against another king, does not sit down first and consider whether he is able with ten thousand to meet him who comes against him with twenty thousand? Or else, while the other is still a great way off, he sends a delegation and asks conditions of peace. So likewise,

whoever of you does not forsake all that he has cannot be My disciple. Salt is good; but if the salt has lost its flavor, how shall it be seasoned? It is neither fit for the land nor for the dunghill, but men throw it out. He who has ears to hear, let him hear!

The cost of being the Church is great, but the rewards are infinitely greater. Life is only fulfilling when we do what we were created to do, when we experience the freedom that only comes in being the Church, the Body of Christ, the Liberating Army of God. We are to live like soldiers to be free and to make people free. Paul in 2 Timothy 2:3-7 commands us:

You therefore must endure hardship as a good soldier of Jesus Christ. No one engaged in warfare entangles himself with the affairs of this life, that he may please him who enlisted him as a soldier. And also if anyone competes in athletics, he is not crowned unless he competes according to the rules. The hardworking farmer must be first to partake of the crops. Consider what I say, and may the Lord give you understanding in all things.

There is a Story at the heart of Creation which concerns *you*, which is about *you* in God's Purposes. Your path to freedom, fulfillment, adventure, love, joy, and real life lies in God's Purpose for you as part of the Church, as His Romance, Body, Family, Temple, Pillar and Ground of the Truth,

Weapon, and Liberating Army. There is no higher purpose or calling for a human being.

"For everyone to whom much is given, from him much will be required; and to whom much has been committed, of him they will ask the more" (Luke 12:48). You, o reader, have been given much by the Lord Jesus, much of which has been examined in what you've read in this book. What will you do with this knowledge for which you are now responsible?

The world needs you. Jesus is calling. Fulfill your part in the Story. Live like a soldier. Be the change. Fight the fight. Free the world. Be the Liberation Front.

THANKS FROM THE AUTHOR

It takes more than a village to raise a book; it takes a city. Those due my thanks are legion. These are a few of those legionaries (the categories overlap...).

Revolutionaries: Alan Powell, Diane Houk, Michael & Tiffany Forth, Artie & Julia Culver, Pat & Brooke Goeke, Brandee & Grayden Greiner, Robert, Johanna & Andrew, Brenda & Gary Gunter, Tony & Sherry Marchant, Heather Hughes, Robert & Heather Maxwell, Dan Harper, Michelle Koester.

Steelers: Liv Wingate, Sandy Scott, George Watson, Obie Gomez.

Diviners: Reagan Cocke, Doug Richnow, Matt Fenlon, Jan Dantone.

Aristoi: Brenda Davidson, Matt Watson.

NewChurchers: Kim, Von, Angel, and Bob Hart, Jeff Hagerlin, Cyndy and Mark Thompson, Rachel and Jeremy Rider.

ArkAngels: Richard Conine, Randy Chez, David Reding.

Episkopos: Wayne Boosahda.

Culters: Brian Baldwin, Zach Meeks, Ethan Marshall.

Mysterium: Heath Behmer, Christina Cricket and Steven David, Josh Ello.

Didaskalos: John Frame, Francis Schaeffer, James Jordan, Herman Dooyeweerd, Cornelius Van Til.

Distancers: George Grant, Kevin Belmonte, Diana Glyer, Doug Wilson, Terry Glaspey.

Special Thanks:

Post Hillers: Publishers Michael Wilson and Anthony Ziccardi, and especially my editor, Melanie Friebel, who was forced to maneuver through any number of textual oddities, yet did so with spirit and grace.

Co-Presbyteros: Frank Hart.

Chalicers: Ryan and Amy Birsinger, Chuck Dotson, Chris Whittington, Adam and Theresa Arvello, Tom Maples, Laura Bogard, Kay Clinton, Dwayne Bohac, and especially Joan Tankersley, who virtually single-handedly engineered this book's publishing.

Familia: Kemper the Elder and Tommye Crabb, John, Charity, Ari, Aiden, Addison, Asheton, Sam, and Dakota Crabb, Mark, Dawna, Cassidy, and Schedel Luitjen, Jennifer Ford, Alex & Tammy Ford.

Massively: Shanna my wife and life, who has sacrificed greatly to encourage and allow my sundry ministries, and is my only earthly home, Maks, who fears no demons, and Beaux, who lives to love.

ALL GLORY AND HONOR TO JESUS CHRIST

To learn more about the message of this book and the ministry and music of Kemper Crabb:
http://www.kempercrabb.net/

ABOUT THE AUTHOR

Kemper Crabb is a contemporary scholar, a dedicated Episcopal priest, a prolific songwriter and recording artist, and a quiet revolutionary. His media impact varies from his PBS special, Downe in Yon Forest, with a viewing audience in the millions, to a series of worship recordings and rock albums shared on early CCM radio. He is now most active in churches and concert halls in Texas. Considered by many a pioneer of Christian music, he has always garnered a following from the faithful. Texas legend Stevie Ray Vaughn, during an appearance on MTV Unplugged, proclaimed Kemper's early release, The Vigil, his favorite record. Known for his bands ArkAngel and RadioHalo, he also joined the radio-popular Caedmon's Call and is now known to many for his popular Medieval Christmas Concerts.

Through all his creative transformations, Kemper has been devoted to Christ and His church. He has studied, served and become a well-respected priest known for his exceptional teaching. His ardor for Christ leads his learning audience to pursue an uncompromising Gospel. He is a sought after teacher in and out of his ordained CEEC community. Deeply committed as an educator in the Classical Charter School community he is helping reform how students view their world. A bold Texan, he has a heritage of evangelism through his father, who has been engaged in foreign missions for over forty years, with two Nobel prize nominations . His passion for Jesus and His church has led Kemper to write this manuscript and engage readers to consider the Church as a revolutionary Liberation Front.